Innocence
Lost in a Black Embrace

Innocence
Lost in a Black Embrace

Edward E Bortot

authorHOUSE®

AuthorHouse™
1663 Liberty Drive
Bloomington, IN 47403
www.authorhouse.com
Phone: 1-800-839-8640

First published by AuthorHouse   09/09/2011

ISBN: 978-1-4634-2660-6 (sc)
ISBN: 978-1-4634-2661-3 (ebk)

Library of Congress Control Number: 2011910313

Printed in the United States of America

Any people depicted in stock imagery provided by Thinkstock are models, and such images are being used for illustrative purposes only.
Certain stock imagery © Thinkstock.

This book is printed on acid-free paper.

Dedication

I would like to thank my lovely wife Kelley Martinez.
I love you more than you will ever know.
I would also like to thank my mother Salli P Bortot who raised me to be the individual
I am today.

Honorable Dedication

Team Fierce

This is dedicated to my trainer and instructor Reggie Mitchell and to the entire Team Fierce. Our training has kept my mind pure, owner of my own soul, and master of my own destiny. Had it not been for training in MMA and Jiu Jitsu my path of destruction would have come to a bitter end. But a new lease on life and different outlook on the human soul gave me confidence and a new-found faith in my abilities in this life.
Thank you!

I would like to thank all family and friends that have helped me and supported me.

Above all else I would like to thank God who gave me a gift to use words to paint pictures. Thank you my heavenly father.

Thank you all

Foreword

This book completes the Innocent Soul trilogies. This book is darker than the other two. It is philosophically deeper. This book represents the conclusion and the end of an Innocent Soul. Know and understand the words spoken in this book and read deep within the message each poem states. These poems reflect people I know, people I see, my imagination, and the world I live in.

Calf Cruncher

How can you hurt someone that is already in pain?
What can you do to jade someone who is already a jaded soul?
How can you inflict emotional torment with someone who welcomes it?
Why would you drive someone to insanity when they reside in insane?
How could you threaten someone with death when they wish for death?
A sickened life with a dark side that dwells in anguish.
A jaded soul that is tainted with blemish's of blackness.
A tortured pen that speaks to his readers through his dark side.

Author's Comments:

This is my pen name

Contents

I. POEMS OF SPIRITUALITY

These poems are about finding your self once again and coming into a new level within yourself. It's about seeing the light and finding redemption. It's about changing your ways and being a better person. I hope that everyone some time in their life can find within themselves the spirituality that can take them to another realm within life.

Within

Rip my flesh from my bone.
Bury me and leave me alone with
premonitions of 18 vision stone.

The unmarked graves of unselfish slaves.
A reminder of dehumanization in back alley caves.
A savior in his mortality who tries to save.

A treason brought fourth on a black day.
A knife in the back that leaves a lasting display.
Two faces of the same individual leading in two different ways.

A faithless fling that sings with protruding force.
A life being a blemish on a disdainful course.
A stoic laughter in silence, trying to find its true source.

The grains of sands run through my hands.
A high stake life with death's demands.
You are no more complex, than I am a simple man.

Cocoon

A brutal Ending to my negative demise.
I am embracing the truth and throwing away the lies.

I have become what I am.
An overachiever and an honorable man.

My true self has been revealed in the end.
The magnitude of the past I amend.

I carry my convictions on my back.
It is my evil past they attack.

I have become a black-winged butterfly
who is now soaring high in the bright blue sky.

My soul is shining as smooth as the sun.
Peace within my self as my new life has begun.

Reaping Wisdom

All my true friends are dead and gone.
My eyes awaken to every break of dawn.

Yet I can't find the reasons why things went wrong.
If I don't find them soon, I don't think I can go on for to long.

All my life strength is slowly draining away.
It is taking its toll and my mind is longing to stray.

They say you don't have to be old to be wise,
yet my true wisdom was attained at an older age before my very eyes.

Every day is a day in which for some reason I live.
Every waking moment is the reflections in which I want to forgive.

Let the sword of Arch-Angel Michael protect me in my time of need.
Let it be the repenting weapon to which I bleed.

Let his wings spread far and wide.
Let him take me under his wing like the ocean tide.

May my heart be reborn with a kindred spirit that runs free.
Let my soul be touched again with God's soft spoken plea.

Old Soul

I have succumbed to death many times.
It is the memories of these past lives that keep me alive.

I am no exception to falling to death.
I am no healer of the faith as I hear their whispers under their breath.

My soul is very old, yet willing to live in many human shells.
It beats being a saint in heaven and burning in everlasting hell.

I die and then I live again.
Don't worry about me as you will always remain my friend.

If you could do what I do then maybe we will see each other again.
Many friendships in this life, the past, and the next, it won't end.

So for now I say goodbye to you in this life we live.
Maybe I will see you in the next life we give.

Conquering Demons

I am devouring serpents in the middle of the street.
I am heaving as I am stuffing them in my mouth to eat.

My demons are being cut down with intense savagery.
I am eating them as I am hostile and angry.

I am conquering my demons from my present and my past.
At the rate I am going they will not last.

They are being slaughtered with no second thoughts.
I ate the last of them as they fought.

I have wiped myself a clean slate.
I have paved myself my own fate.

It is my destiny to control.
This is my life now, this is my soul.

Re-Invented

I count the minutes to my death.
I monitor the broken words being spoken under my breath.

My blood red lips made a lasting impression.
My downfall holds dear to my depression.

I have countless actions of retribution.
I have a disregard to meaningless illusion.

I run beyond the depths of hell.
My mind to keep, my soul to sell.

I tread where eagles dare.
My actions are proposals for what is fair.

My life is slowly draining away.
This life I leave to commit to a new life and a new day.

Spirituality Found

I am egocentric in my dark convictions.
My evil actions have been given notice to their evictions.

The sun shines bright on me on this day.
My mind clouded no longer as I kneel and pray.

I ask God the father for forgiveness in my time of need.
I ask that he grant me the right life to lead.

My sadness has left for now to fight me again another day.
Yet for now my happiness and I are together at play.

For once I can see with clarity.
For once I can feel my sincerity.

My mind and soul together as one.
To another level of existence I have become.

Open Heart

I run through fiery flames of pain.
I felt her physical presence as she came.

The touch of her hand heals with passion,
yet she can only heal in small rations.

Her love is from the eloquent kind.
If you search, it is her pure heart you will find.

Her sincerity is her strength.
She exemplifies it always at great length.

Her glow is of innocence in stature.
Her smiling touch gives your human shell giving rapture.

She is the sender of the good.
The healer of the weak
and when you see her you will realize
her presence is not misunderstood.

Beyond Time

It has been a year; yet it is only tomorrow.
Tomorrow was today.
As today is only yesterday.

Deliverer of Pain

Actions that move faster.
A swift sense of disaster.
A flood that runs through it.
A movement that is quiet.
A touch that changes to another way.
A transformation that dances to a different sway.
A submission of diligence.
A giver back to intelligence.
A taker of suffering.
To the endlessness of pain we submit.

Heaven or Hell?

Walking above the depths of hell.
Walking below the heavens above.
Both vie and try to secure my soul.
Which one will it be?
Sometimes hell seems to be my heaven.
Yet it is my heaven that sometimes is my hell.
I am a free agent in this tug of war.
Which one can offer me the best?
My soul for now, for later my soul to sell.

Author's Comments:

"The choice is ours to choose."

Purpose

A soul that has been branded a fool.
A fool that has been deemed a condemned soul.
A spirit in search of a purpose.

God the Father

Did I not give you love?
Did I not do the small things that matter?
Did I not give you appreciation for who you are?
Did I not believe in you in your time of need?
Have I not been kind?
Have I not shown you how humble I am?

I remember displaying all of these and so I have been taken for granted.

Remember Me

Walking on hollow ground
while submerging in a grave of a rotting sound.

An army of rotting decay corpses fills the void.
They pull themselves under in attempt from the world they can avoid.

Insidious in their nature they come with silence in their stature.
Their lost souls that scream to the world in an attempt for them to capture;

to capture the meaning they lost in the essence of their existence.
They seek the approval of the living for their assistance.

For remembrance keeps the soul alive in death while maintaining their presence.
Remembrance is what keeps them alive
and it is their soul that flourishes with memories before them it presents.

Fusion

The opposite that attracts.
A wisdom that melts with honesty.
Two different faces seen as one.
A new direction.
A new entity created out of two.

Still Life

A breeder of hate.
A conception of anger that denies happiness.
Emotional turmoil that turns sour.
A sour taste that resembles ugly.
An image that portrays violence.
Bleeding the innocence from good.
A fountain of clear water that spawns a wrongful pleasure.
A filter that burns the positive and reeks the negative.
A life that is wasted in its evil doings.
A comatose that is not living, nor dead.

Master of Souls

My recollections of violence have passed me by.
I have no more love, only remorseless remains.
My remedy is the growing seed in which it cries out in vain.

I am methodical in my means to justify the ends.
I inherit a dastardly vision that lays waste to my unselfish friends.
I am thee defector of wrong as the evil I try to fend.

My resiliency keeps me strong in my self-belief.
It is the soul at the end of the tree that purges thee embattled leaf.
It burns softly in the light wind in which it is to cease.
I am a commander in the sense of a soul that has been released.

Spiritual Escort

At the rainbow's edge is where you will find me.
A silence in the wind is the cover that defines me.

The sprinkle of water breaks me down to the bare essentials.
It brings me strength and makes me multi-dimensional.

The clouds are the shields that protect me and provide me safe harbor.
It leaves her vulnerable and with this, the crowd mobs her.

I strike down with lightening with furious vengeance by my side.
It is the crowd that disperses; it is the crowd that divides.

She runs to me with desperate confessions.
My kiss to her sucks her life's essence.

I am her spiritual guide.
I will now take her to the next life she will find.

Mirror

A defeating fashion rests at its core.
A depleting brash assassin they adore.

A demon spawned from the belly of the witch.
An imperative death wiped clean from a tainted bitch.

A rise of conformity that exists in our minds.
A fallen soldier who was divided over time.

A tranquil world left to humanity.
A satanic realm that exists in insanity.

Wisdom reaps the gifts of old.
Ignorance created the habits that are cold.

Sifting through eternal forests of dedication.
Waning through jungles of meditation.

Where there is one there is the opposite waiting.
Conformity to disbanding with the ugly side hating.

Blinding Light

Drifting through a mystic stream while submerging myself in a deep dream.
It is the reverse of the tide that has shown me to run and hide.

It is the wave of darkness that tries to drown me with simple means.
It is the drift tide that comes at me like evil fiends.

There is no one here to save me from the desecration of the soul.
It was an outburst that turned to anger and then spun wickedly out of control.

The sun is rising out of the ashes of the ocean blue.
It is bringing a rebirth and my only thought is of you.

The gleaming light turns my eyes blind.
Yet for once in this jaded life I can finally see and truly find.

It is the reflections of a soul that speaks to the heavens above.
It is the memories that have lapsed and it is the heart that has turned into love.

The hate is gone and with it the anger has sang its last song.
I feel no pain or misery and my will not go on for to long.

My innocence has been restored and faithful I will be.
A new found life that has opened my heart and made my soul free.

What is This Life For?

To God

We are given life and then it is taken away.
Are we mere pawns in a proving life?
Proving ourselves worthy to be in the gates of heaven?
We are given this life to prove ourselves and then it is taken away?
So I say, why give me life at all? Then there would be no death.
Let my soul be stored and life not be given to me so that I may not fall.
What a cruel game that is played at our expense.

Disguised

The spirit calls the beckoning of the will.
The will that protrudes in the deafening sound of the kill.

A fallen angel who mourns his new found destiny.
A forest of death that moves through the ebony of infamy.

The infinite wisdom that resides in the oceans of the mind.
A cynic who cries in the waters of emotions that are intertwined.

Golden wings that spread for flight.
It is the success that embarks on its granted right.

A fallacy that justifies the truth in its entity.
The face that emerges that reveals its true identity.

Ride the Lightening

I crack the dark sky with a whisper in my eye.
The stars are my guide as I use the wind to fly.

The black rain pours hard and fast with a soothing brisk.
The thunder pounds across the land with a moving whisk.

The tracers of my soul can be seen from afar.
My view is of me moving as fast as a shooting star.

Life released me and shot me in the dark.
Death embraced me as I lit the spark.

My journey is unknown to all, for only I will know.
I ride the lightening of life after death as I break past life's plateau.

Who Are We?

These given rules make us mere fools who need to dwell in sin.
We extricate our souls for the relish of our greedy goals while living under plastic skin.
The smiles come with life's trials in which we try to win.
We embellish our defeats while trying to maintain our dignity deep within.

Our eyes glaze the riff while our heart cries.
It is our slow demise that runs with purity as one dies.
It is the wise that run and hide during the formation of the black skies.
Hypnotize with deceitful eyes that ponder their dirty little lies.

Looking inside ourselves to the person we do not know.
Being helplessly picked apart by the hungry black crow.
Looking in the mirror with the reflection of a stranger climbing beyond their plateau.
Our true selves we long to show.

Self-Existence

My journey is to get to heaven before the sun goes down.
It is this path of self-existence I have found.

It is the destination of where I need to be that is known.
It is the journey that is the mystery that is not shown.

I repelled the wicked people whose existence is to cause strife.
I have amused myself in my convictions of seeking a better life.

She came to me with a kiss of repression.
I left her in a world of regression.

I left the old and went with the new.
I do not regret my flaws as with them I am through.

I do not look back, but rather look ahead.
I found my self-existence in a world that is dead.

Ghosts

I remember rising above my body in a most uncomfortable way.
It was a feeling of losing my self in the mixture of the fray.
When I awoke there was blackness with a shining light as bright as a sunny day.
I spoke as you could see my breath as I exhaled in a most frightening way.

The path was paved with thorns that went to the light.
It was my feelings and emotions that I had to fight.
The fear of the unknown left me sulking within delight.
The delight of knowing that I was on some kind of unimaginable flight.

They welcomed me with open arms as they had no faces.
I was disturbed and perturbed as I asked what this place is.
They whispered with soft voices as they blessed me with their graces.
I soon found myself overwhelmed with their embarking embraces.

I longed to get away as I ran back to the blackness.
I ran across the thorns toward my awaken distress.
I felt pounding and pulling that was moving my chest.
I heard voices saying he is coming back and yelling god bless.

My eyes opened to physicians and nurses that were surrounding me.
They said I had died and that God answered their plea.
I asked them, "Where are the people with no faces and the thorns of debris?"
They gave me a puzzled look as I knew now they were the ghosts that had been set
free.

Stigmata

Death stalks as evils abound.
It radiates an essence of a hissing sound.

The hand that grasps my throat with great force
is the hand that embarks upon a trail of remorse.

Life is squeezed from the portions of vile.
It is the stark look that brings a killer's smile.

It is the embodiment of an act of pain.
It seeks the reaction of a simple gain.

The blood runs down the hands of the innocent one.
A reminder of the pain that bore the sins of man that was to be done.

A simple teardrop of blood that runs deep.
It is the eyes of misery that begins to seep.

This Life

To those that did not ask to be here

I say to you all that life is overrated.
It is nothing more than work and it leaves me agitated.

I did not ask to be here.
It wasn't out of fear.

Who gave them the right?
To make my soul the gift of flight.

I say to you this life is overrated.
It is nothing more than a world for a slave as I have overstated.

I would rather have stayed from where I came, then to be here.
What gave them the right to put me in this shell as I have made myself clear.

This life is a pillar of a false image to which I deny.
It is this life that does not forgive to which I dam the sky.

So I say to you all, life is overrated as I already stated.
It is an entity to which I did not give my permission to be created.

The Crow

A medium between the living and the dead.
It is the belief of a spirit that pulls ahead.

Its black embrace is a welcomed face.
It's potent pace brings acknowledgment of its trace.

They fly with conviction to let the living know.
What once was is now, and they long to show.

Their soul flies high in a crimson sky with a shining glow.
Their spirit burns bright with flight inside the black crow.

DeAtH

They say Death is the end.
I say Death is only the beginning.
It is a release from this life we live.
It is a gateway to another realm.
It is the beginning of something new.
Something that cannot be explained.
Only through Death will we know.

II. POEMS OF INSPIRATION AND HOPE

These poems are about winning in life and in death. They are about the individual who succeeds when they have been knocked down. They are about the person who refuses to give up, but purges on into victory. May they always be blessed.

Picking Myself Up Off The Floor

My fortitude is withering away in a melting stay.
My spirit begs for empathy as my soul is to lay.
I have laid here and endured emotional pain.
This emotional pain has almost driven me to insane.
Yet I forge on to find my self again and again.
It is my self that has appeared to be a new-found friend.
Every time my head is above water I find myself drowning.
This water is overwhelming and my lungs are taking a pounding.
For some reason my will to live will not let me die.
Once again it proves that my soul is meant to fly.
I am a determined soul to make it in this hard world.
I am always found in the deepest of waters, only to be discovered as a black pearl.
My desire will not let me down.
My wings were not meant for the ground.
I will always rise again every time someone chooses to knock me down.

Oppression of Fear

Falling into oblivion with nothing more to spare.
It is the essence of life and death that I truly dare.
You dare me to die.
It is you I defy.

I will kill when being killed.
I will fight till I am truly filled.
I will die when I am dy-ing.
I will know I have succeeded when I see you crying.

Your eyes of despair leave me waning in my empty soul.
Yet it is your heart that has made me whole.
You're a fool of fools who wander away from the care.
Yet your quite content with the pain to which you cannot bear.

Wandering in and out of obscurity to the reckoning.
It is you that leaves your shadow here for the beckoning.
Swimming through muddy waters to get to the clear.
It is your will that has broken your underlying fear.

Humanitarian

I am keeper who finds.
A revolutionary who makes a difference.
I am an advocate of change.
A lobbyist for an improved way.
I am a loyalist at heart.
A soldier that picks apart.
I am a soothing soul.
A one hit wonder who takes his toll.
I am exorcist of misery.
I am a proponent for humanity.

Looking Past the Individual

To people who don't see the real person in front of them

I am a rainbow in the frigid dark.
It is these colors in which I will make my mark.
I am running through a stream of imagination.
I am drinking water of transformation.
I am looking beyond what is in front of me.
My eyes can see past the vision that has hindered me.
My spells are spellbound with consumption.
I do not make decisions prescribed on assumptions.
To everyone else life is moving fast.
Yet to me it is in slow motion in which it is the test I pass.
I confess that I am not of the norm.
People even say that I am the eye of the storm.
I can't deny who I am.
I am above the rest in this mortal land.
I run with wolves to be part of the pack.
I swim with sharks so that I can bring my killer instincts back.
I am everything you want me to be.
I am your lover, your sinner, whoever stands before you of what you want to see.

Educator

To all Educators that make a difference in their student's lives

I give from the heart in a desperate attempt to get to heaven.
I am an overachiever in the sense I want to be represented by the number seven.
I give so that others can have new-found opportunity.
It is my conscious that succumbs to my sincerity.
I want to see others succeed.
I am tired of watching society bleed.
I hope they find a self-sense of liberty.
I hope it is a freedom of their mind that becomes a reality.
I give them education in an attempt that they have a bright future.
I hope that knowledge will be their power when they mature.
I hope that their mind will never carry boundaries.
I hope that it is never closed and they find answers to their inquiries.
I hope the new freedom they find is the education of their mind.
I hope the life they live is lived with the happiness from the education they find.

Facing the Past that Consumes You

A founder of truth who left the fallacies behind.
Her new beginning is her new self she finds.
She has overcome trials and tribulations during her life.
She has seen both sides of the protruding knife.
Her experiences of pain have made her strong.
It is her past she leaves and with this she won't see the pain for to long.
For once she is doing something for herself.
With this she finds inner wealth.
She has conquered the issues that have consumed her.
She has faced her skeletons that were the inquiring inside observer.
She now stands as an inspiring example of one that has over come.
She made it in this world and now she never has to run.

Fractured

Their wicked lies that I have despised have hurt me so.
They take me down to burn,
yet it is the touch of their toxin that sours my soul.

Their lovable smiles are killers hiding behind them.
It is their cold stare that shakes me and sends them.

It sends them in a frenzy of hate with a massacres scene.
It is this peccancy that brings to life this beautiful hate machine.

They attack my emotions with a vivid malice.
They seek my will for the breaking, which represents callous.

They have left me with my emotions to soak in.
For I have only been fractured and not broken

Author's Comments:

"Rumors and lies can hurt you, but cannot break you."

Patrick

My life was fast and I didn't care if I lived or died.
Yet when you see someone close to you who dies; you begin to fear death.
A cold feeling burns inside you.
It makes you see within the premonitions of life.
You begin to see life in another state of mind.
You realize you have not fully lived the life you have been granted.
Your self-actualization of this precious gift makes you want to live again.
The honest life you live; the fear of death begins to fade away.
You truly learn to live life and death becomes obsolete.
Through Patrick's death he gave me life.
I will love him while he is gone and I will live life until we see each other once again,
my beautiful friend,
Patrick.

When No One Else Believes

Everyone looks at you with questions.
They have that look of doubt.
They don't believe you can do it.
Some even want you to fail.
That's when you look deep within yourself.
You find that inner you that doesn't doubt you.
Then when you achieve, when you win, when you overcome,
you can say I believed when no one else did.
I believed in myself.
I believed in my skills.
I believed in me.

Aspiring

I reach with ambition to be the man I am.
I push with pure strength to become my biggest fan.

My self-confidence has been cracked with emotion.
My self-esteem has held its own with great devotion.

I am searching for the confidence with the wind at my side.
I am confiding to the insolence in which it is to define.

My despair is my vanity that displays my sanity.
It is the wisdom that reaps that flows inside of me.

I am the one who reached deep inside to be alive.
I am the man that will get there, as it is my strong will that has arrived.

Assurance

I seduce you with thoughts of promise.
I give you a sense of self-belief.
I pick you up from off the floor.
I give you hope for brighter futures.
I point to a better way to live this life.
I believe in you that you can do these things.
Then as swift as I came into your life,
I am gone.

Embraced

Your soft skin relieves the pain that dwells within.
Your immense sensual touch caresses my senses with pleasurable euphoria.
The tip of your tongue brings sensations of chills that run through my body.
Your red silky hair I run my fingers through with a soft passionate kiss that touches
those full luscious lips.
I begin to slowly kiss your body down by your neck and then close to your breasts.
Your fingertips slightly run up and down my body with exploration behind its madness.
Then we engage, and we are two bodies that are intertwined with a long lasting
pleasure.
The sensations of the feelings are exploding throughout us.
We kiss with fire that burns throughout our overlapping bodies.
Through the night we go on until we lie naked to ourselves.
Still intertwined, falling into a pleasurable sleep.

Shipwrecked

A heartless fool whose heart has been shipwrecked.
A meaning in simplicity that is constantly pecked.

The fool tries to see through the broken waters.
This fool can sense the blood of the innocent being slaughtered.

Their emotions being squeezed with hurt.
Their heart trying to heal while staying alert.

They seek for compensation by engaging in wreck less intimacy.
Yet without the emotional attachment it is nothing more than physical irresponsibility.

The love that was, is far too gone.
It was a relationship that had gone on for to long.

Now running from loneliness in its empty corridor.
It has nothing left in their shipwrecked heart to store.

Reflections from within this fool's heart,
is a search for a new island to sail with a new start.

Your Reflections of Pain

In your face I see reflections of pain.
It is so immense I am surprised it has not turned you insane.

Your eyes are windows to the thorns you wear.
It is this haunting past that gives you your frigid stare.

It is your demeanor you created through your dark experiences you experienced.
It is this pain you kept hidden and nicely incensed.

You are alive, yet you walk around dead.
These reflections of pain are unforgiving in your head.

You are nothing more than a broken soul demanding redemption.
Yet you must let go, mend your soul with defining reflection.

Shining Through

I have become an example of shinning good.
If I could be better, than you know I would.

I have had many set backs in my life yet I have overcome.
I have risen above and joined myself as one.

I choose not to look back, but rather look ahead.
I leave the sunsets and look towards the sunrise instead.

My brutal past has left me dry with a lonely tear in my eye.
My present is currently riding a high and to my past I have said goodbye.

My future holds a promising life.
I will never forget so that I may not return to strife.

In the meantime I help those that help themselves.

Finder of Redemption While Crawling in the Dark

I cannot see and the blind I foresee.
I fathom my life's blood is draining away as I plea.

Plea for a way to get out of this lonely scene.
A victim who fell to the spoils of war to a dark fiend.

Breaking down the walls of Jericho with a smile.
Emptying my sin with portions that are vile.

These feelings in my soul have left only to return another day.
I found the light for now and this is where my heart yearns to stay.

Belief in Myself

To people who truly believe in themselves

My vision has been clouded with sinners.
Yet I remain valiant in my convictions to be the ultimate winner.

My soul is jaded and black with sickness that is now faded.
I smile with redemption knowing that I upgraded.

I am an animal with the instincts of a big jungle cat.
My growl is heard throughout this urban plain that is flat.

This is my world for me to rise and take it.
This is my realm with me to confide and make it.

I know what I am and I know where I am going.
I know that my success and my writing will keep my good will flowing.

The belief in my self is what makes me unique.
I am filled with riches like an old expensive antique.

I will stay where I need to stay and remain above the rest.
I know deep inside me that I am truly blessed.

Rising

Living in oblivion with cracked confidence.
Seeing is believing with mirrors of indifference.

Finding within myself the person I use to know.
It is this person that brings the happiness with a glow.

I swallow the last drop of pride that has been drained.
Sensing the skeletons from the demons as they march on with their parade.

I am looking to extricate these skeletons as they begin to show.
I am looking past the flowers of the markers that are hidden below.

I will face these demons with my confidence shining through.
I will beat them once again as I am a proven winner with a confidence that is new.

Lost in Imprisonment

Finding redemption in the lost souls of pain,
their faces are imprinted and burned inside my brain.

Their cries are of the hollow kind.
It is the sins that bore a sensitive mind.

A wish that speaks a fool's prison.
It is the acts of benevolence that have arisen.

These souls will not leave without a caring grace.
They reemerge in my dreams with a lasting embrace.

They seek freedom inside from a caring mind.
It is this new freedom they hope to find.

My Keeper

You have given me strength that I did not know I had.
You kept me warm in a cold world that held me sad.

You lifted me up to the sky.
It was your soft touch and caress that made me cry.

It was the true meaning of love I saw in both your eyes.
You have taken my heart to another level of high.

You handle me with great care.
It is your love that I truly dare.

Dare to keep it in this life and the next.
Keep our relationship simple and avoid the complex.

I appreciate who you are.
I hold you to my heart as I am truly being sincere from a far.

My love for you can never die,
for my love for you is strong and it can only multiply.

Worn Tiger

They say a tiger never changes his stripes.
Yet the stripes displayed on me are battle scars of life's gripes.

They are embedded in a stain of pleasure that is misused.
They are printed and tattooed on me that leave me battered and bruised.

Yet when someone tries to pull me down, they do not succeed.
It is these stripes that are displayed with honor in the sense of my good and bad deeds.

They carry with me life's victories and defeats.
They leave me bitter and happy that fills my life with an emotional sweet.

I find these stripes imprinted on me the challenges to which I had to compete.
The things I have seen and the things that I have done can only leave me more complete.

Wiped Clean

I have washed away the pain that accompanied me.
I am here to murder the world free from tyranny.
The precious gift of self-righteousness has failed me.
It has allured me into a prison of illusion.
What was real is not.
What was not was real.
Now it is time to bare the pain.
Endure the wonder of what happiness is.

ReD

Your red hair runs smoothly through my fingers.
Your green eyes bring me pleasure.
The touch of your skin leaves me breathless.
The way your finger tips run across my skin takes me to euphoria.
The soft touch of your lips remind me of the missed 20 years.
I gently bite your neck and hear your sensuous moan.
Your mind I admire with great satisfaction and respect.
Our conversations go on for miles.
I took you for granted long ago.
Yet today, I appreciate who you truly are.

Follow

If I asked you to be with me, would you follow?
Would you carry with me your dreams and emotions instead of being hollow?

Could you trust in me your affection that I would not leave?
Do your eyes see honesty and know that I would never let you grieve?

Can you see the affection and sincerity when I gaze into your eyes?
Do you know that when we make love you leave me hypnotized?

Do you know the powerful words of, "I love you", makes me feel good inside?
Do you know that if you just said those words to say them that I would die?

Can you imagine your life without me?
Did I tell you my heart is a three—lock box and only you hold the key?

I have traveled the earth and you are the only woman who understands the true me.
Some have pretended and displayed their false show, but your heart is true and this I
can see.

Your smile of affection truly captures the essence of you.
Your lips they speak of the impressions I construe.

I know you love me because your true affections come shining through.
So I say as I speak to those beautiful green eyes, thank you.

III. POEMS OF SORROW, PAIN, AND LOSS

These poems are about hard emotions that come from losing someone or something to death or a relationship. It is about emotional pain that accompanies the loss we feel. It is about people we see endure the pain and misery and no matter what we do to help, they refuse.

False Sense of Security

Variations of a demeaning value.
A deceiving mind that represents shallow graves.
Moving objects that sway as they move vividly.
A captured emotion that will not be released.
A captivating sound that you cannot hear.
Horrid visions that remain hidden behind unseen.
An comfortable feeling that cannot be felt.
Pain that is seen; but not endured.
A sense of security; yet it is not secure.
To false premonitions we become.

Broken Morals

A blemish on my life.
A stain on my heart.
My ethics and morals are being pulled apart.
Soft words being spoken from the start.
Whispers being shattered in the end.
This unfilled end has become my lonesome friend.
It is the spoiled sin I recommend.
Its looks are deceiving.
Its taste is delirious in its meaning.
I have become a watered down notion.
My benevolence is my undying devotion.

Vindication

Drowning in a lake of transgression.
Living in a world of suppression.
Trying to make my mark in this world a lasting impression.

Raising high a fist of rage.
A beast moving beyond the confinements of its cage.
Rising to the occasion on a worldly stage.

Finding a lost moment intertwined in mass confusion.
A slipknot of reality engaging in diffusion.
A ring of illusion reeking diabolical delusion.

A brigade of disarray.
A face that displays dismay.
A violation of unreadily delay.

A wicked life that feeds immoral.

Eyes Wide Shut

There is no denying my good will and irrefutable ways of the life I live.
I walk in the light of the dark in which it is the twist of irony I give.

I seize the moment only to not be denied.
It is my secrecy that is mistaken for trying to pretend I lied.

The tension builds with anger and the fire in my eye.
It is my vigorous ways that I try to deny.

My greatest blunders are the mistakes that make me wonder.
It is my bombastic expressions that will drown me and take me under.

My soporific demeanor leaves me vulnerable for the taking.
It is these horrific dreams that bring me to my eternal awakening.

Running Away

Their insinuations are taking their toll.
They punctured my existence as it has lured out of control.

I grimace in pain with an urgency to live.
It is a symbolic gesture instead that I give.

This transformation has made me irate.
It is their prefabrication I run away from and try to deviate.

My prudence has left my side.
It is their demeanor that I try to divide.

This burden is mounting the pressure in my head.
If it amounts any longer I will be face down and dead.

Hidden Agenda

They have no reason, no hate, no love.
They come from dire straights and from the heavens above.

What have I done?
What have I become?
Where did these influential devils come from?

I was a mere pawn in their lucrative game.
It was the temptation they filled into my vein.
It was their curiosity that caught my name.

Their eyes were filled with unpromising compromise.
Yet it was only a lie and it was their agenda that rose with the outlying sunrise.

Their intentions were filled with the cruel intentional kind.
It was these mutilators that twisted my innocent mind.

They came with hope and left me with misery.
They laughed and cried at the belittled scenery.

They came in the light and left in the dark.
It was their unprovoked violence that took to the spark.

I fell to my knees and asked, "What has become me?"
The sky broke apart and thundered, "You are a prisoner of envy!"

Suicide

The life I live I am not happy in.
As hard as I try it seems I can never win.
I am contemplating committing the ultimate sin.
I have tried other alternatives, but this decision has come from within.
The consequences are tragic I know.
It was the inner me I tried to show.
I am to be driven to eternal damnation.
Being eternally ripped apart in condemnation.
I am a soul lost in misery.
A heart that cries in capture of a hidden conspiracy.
My last breath takes it toll.
It is my selfishness that went out of control.
I leave this world with my last dying parting groan.

Sanitarium

The faster I move the quicker you burn.
The more I try to help, the more your soul will return.

Your haunting cries scare the scattered ravens from their nesting ground.
Your pain is heard through a cold world filled with misery while making no sound.

They watch you with fascination as they study your reactions.
They seek an understanding while ignoring the distractions.

They seek the rationale behind your insanity.
This is their way of giving to humanity.

Yet they don't understand your pain.
They do not see the visions of the insane.

This is the place for you to live out your madness.
Yet when we see you we cry with sadness.

Mental Hospital

Further regressing back into time.
My mind is diminishing and I cannot find a gleaming shine.
My life is spotless in the way of regression.
Yet I find myself back in the ways of transgression.
I look deep into what the messages say, yet I am a non believer in what they portray.
I have become disjointed in a world gone wrong.
It is my world that I speak of that seems to go on for to long.
I fight and then I lose, but most times I win.
I try to live with a pure heart, but my habit is too long to sin.
I wear my emotions inside myself.
This is my demise and the reason for my poor health.
I am insane with a knack for curious.
It is the game I play with intentions that are serious.
No one knows who I am.
I sit here in silence playing the innocent lamb.
I stare in a gaze with no emotions to display.
The same routine, but a different day.

Disassociation

The horror of long ago still haunts me today.
They are like dreams to me, yet they happened.
They keep appearing like flash backs that refuse to leave.
They keep getting in my way of progress.
It is a bridge that it seems I cannot get over.
It is blocking my life and the life of others.
Every day I pray so that I may not see a new day.
Yet it comes just like the next day and the day after.
I wish this life would carry me away.
Take me somewhere confined from the pain and misery.
The haunting will not stop and the flash backs turn into dreams.
The dreams turn into past memories.
The memories turn into reality.
The reality is the horror and abuse that will not leave me.

Confrontation From Within

The dark clouds make a black swirl in the sky.
It covers the moon, for it is the light it defies.

Incensed with immense passion for the taking.
The inevitable succumbing to sin for the breaking.

Bare to the world for all to know.
A hollow ground for all to show.

Diverse embellishment of the weak kind.
Various disturbing acts of a sick mind.

Persuasive whispers that ask for terror.
Coercive demons that lay in their lair.

The dilemma of red evil has been spilled.
The sage of emotions are laying in the killing fields that are being filled.

Repulsive scenes with visuals of the twisted.
Their defective nature is the killing they assisted.

They are subject to falling.
The demons are pulling and crawling.

Black as night with the wicked trying to lure you in sight.
No more rolling with yourself as you go on with your inner fight.

Love Kills

Love is a sick pleasure that is disguised as misery.
It gives you full of promise and plays on your sympathy.

It induces you with feelings of happiness and sincerity.
Yet it leaves you with hate and a desire to lose your apathy.

The one true person you long to be with
has left you with an ugly taste under your breath.

They came to you as an angel in a white glistened gown.
Yet they left like a demon with despair as their crown.

The enchanted feelings you had in the beginning turned to pain.
The sorrow was endured and this word called love almost drove you insane.

Things between you and they that were said were never meant to be.
A sick game of love called misery that unleashed the ugliness to be set free.

Lies and deceit always accompanies the misery with a sorrowful ending.
It is the pain and sorrow that begins as love, but only leaves you empty and fending.

I Use To Love Her

I use to love her with immense passion and feeling.
I use to adore her looks with great admiration.

I lay awake at night thinking of our late night conversations.
I remember her touch.
The memory of her soft spoken words still rise inside me.

Her eyes that looked at me with confidence are a faded memory.
I remember how she held me.
I recall us both saying we wanted this moment to last forever.

The words from her lips said we would be together for evermore.
I remember her laugh.
She is now in the past and so I use to love her.

Walking Along a Thin Line

Living in oblivion at the edge of the burning sun.
A wisdom that is searched before it is begun.

A turning point in time that elapses with passion.
A fast decision made with small portions and rations.

A sight that portrays good on the outside.
Yet it dwells in evil on the inside it confides.

A screeching yell that whistles with the wind.
An army of darkness that dwells in bitter sin.

A caged soul that defies the good it confronts.
It fends it off with malnutrition of a wicked hunt.

A hunter who turned into the prey.
A sick game of give and take that got caught in the fray.

Martyrdom

I am confronting a soft brutal emotional beating.
It is the kind that sets me apart from the norm.
I am the quiet silent type with my defiant nature yearning to come out.
My emotional turmoil is a pain that sucks me dry.
I have no energy, no thought process to go on.
This burden is death stalking me until I succumb to the misery.
Yet for some unknown reason my soul longs for the pain.
I have had it so long it has become my fix.
It truly wears my body down.
Yet my mind hungers for more.
It needs it to thrive in reality.
Death is not an option, but an escape from my addiction.
Yet it is the addiction that keeps me going.
It is the pain that leaves me to live.

Thief of Hearts

Did it dawn on you that I am your obsession?
You can't live without my love and affection.

Our union began with a kiss.
Yet behind my motive was a serpent's hiss.

All your thoughts I consumed.
And my love for you, you assumed.

I was here to blow your mind away from the very start.
I was here to prance in the night and steal your heart.

You never met an individual like me.
That's why your love for me was well conceived.

I became your best friend.
I became your lover and confidant to the end.

I gave you physical pleasure beyond belief.
You said the things you did with me were way beneath.

Way beneath the line in which I made you feel fine.
I took your heart and made you mine as you took me to divine.

Now that I left, you are in misery.
Yet you were the one that set me free.

I came like a thief in the night from the heavens above.
Don't you know I am the thief that stole your love.

Withering Pain

To Patrick Gabriel

On January 2, 2004 I had a dream of death.
I awoke while on a flight while pondering under my breath.

The late night phone call let me know that you were gone.
You were left all alone and it left me feeling withdrawn.

The emptiness filled me with despair.
It left me feeling helpless and this I could not bear.

I asked God the father to bring you back.
Your loss left me in the cold and mourning in black.

Now, it will be three years since you left.
My feelings are left rolling in and out of bereft.

Had I known you would die alone,
I would have left with you engaging in 19 vision stone.

Author's Comments:

"Just thinking of you Patrick"

Changing Sides

The irrelevance of these preceding have me in a bind.
Yet it is a new birth of transgression I find.

I sit and sift through a mystic illusion in my guard.
It is the accomplishment of the mind that I disregard.

Their vapid characteristics are pre-dominate in their own way.
They entice you to beg, they invite you to play.

It is irrelevant to think they are part of the formation.
Yet they exemplify a strong united nation.

I refrain from uncovering my devious past.
I am a replica of good that is moving to fast.

I see beyond the blood red land.
It is the sickness of the sand that sticks to my hand.

The time has passed with a wicked stance.
My true nature abandoning me with an evil dance.

Crossing the Rift

I have been bled from my life source.
I need a transfusion to start me on a different course.

I need the energy to carry on.
I will use it to see beyond.

See beyond the crimson skies
and the individuals who defy.

Defy the rules of life and sin.
Living it everyday and living it to win.

They seek inside themselves a darkness that is revealed.
They open up images and emotions that have been concealed.

They are back and forth over the line we call life.
They have broken dreams
as it seems
to be the norm in this unbroken scene.

A Conscious Absent

You have gutted me to no return.
You have violated me and now I am forever to burn.

Your bad intentions they came shining through.
You're a pig with nothing more to gain, but living on as life's branded fool.

Your emotions are dark, morbid, and cruel.
Yet you walk with confidence as you give off a false portrayal of abiding by the rules.

Your infractions are of the desolate kind.
It is the tool that remanufactures your twisted mind.

Your simple violent actions destroyed a family.
It was your selfishness that didn't think about life's assembly.

You destroyed lives through your irresponsibility.
No conscious, no guilt, no inner social mobility.

You are a waste of a human shell.
Your soul belongs to the demons whom you where spawned by in hell.

Lost Within Myself

An ocean of emotion floods my senses.
Its power that overwhelms me leaves me defenseless.

It gives me feelings of disarray with actions that cause wrath.
I try to swim for safety in order for me to carve a new path.

The loss is demanding in which it stands.
I have been placed in an awkward situation by another's demands.

These feelings are slowly going out with the tide.
They are draining away from me and my life I will continue to abide.

It is doom I have avoided with a serious brush.
Yet the confrontation is unfinished yet I see it turning to rust.

Life goes on with questions I must ponder.
These questions I must answer or forever I will be left to wander.

Wander a world of illusion portraying reality.
Succumbing to the misery of accepting my individuality.

Black Treason

Burning whispers being heard in a cold world.
Tear drops of bleeding solitude with torment that is curled.

A seething salutation that rips through a peaceful act.
A touch of death that is seen in a rear view mirror that is cracked.

A kiss from an apprentice of Judas who resides in the abyss.
A notion of blindness that dwells in an underworld bliss.

Words spoken from the tongue of a demon with a smile.
The fire that burns with wickedness that consumes with vile.

A snake that slides on its belly in the shadows for its' waiting strike.
A heart-ache of misery who loves pain to which they like.

Truth that is revealed in the end of waning sin.
A dark secret that is unfolded with false flesh that represents
the emphatic skin.

Failure

Lurking in despair through my closed window.
A feeling of being down in a broken scene.
A lonely vision of wisdom that abandons me.
I aim to keep my life in order to find the prize.
I am a failure of trying to show individuals there is a better way.
I could not break the narrow-minded cycle of living in misery.
I sulk in a loss of not full filling redemption when it was needed.
It came and then it left as it displayed its ugly face.

Author's Comments:

"Even though we try to help people live a better life, it is the life they live they perceive as normal. But then again what is the norm? Is it our expectations?"

Grounded

I saw a true heart, but I ignored the darkness.
For it was the darkness that consumed them.
They walked in the shadows of life.
They didn't ever reach their full potential.
They never seem to reach the person whom they were meant to be.
They keep themselves grounded never to fly.
They accept their mediocrity as success,
never becoming nothing more than their present form.

Dining on Misery

Feasting on misery is what they say.
It is the wisdom I crave in a most subtle way.

These thoughts are buried in emotion, which leaves me drained.
They take me away to another day leaving me stained.

I know one day they will go away,
but these emotions seem to long to stay.

I reach deep within to do away with this blasphemy.
But it runs through my veins with the ugliness that is in me.

These stains are of disarray that went a stray.
It is thy God that I look above to pray.

I am quick to the quickening of a self-reflection.
It is the true self I see with deep-rooted perception.

A Dark Soul That Failed To Show Her The Light

His Dark Soul came from the depths below.
He lost control and it is his sadistic nature that took its toll.

His eyes wore the reflection of pain that was tortured from the butcher's rain.
It came slowly over the course of time that was left in a brutal domain.

His heart is missing from his ghostly soul.
It was left to die in an emotional state that dug its own hole.

The hurt that reaps within will not let him go.
He has been spoiled with black sin and he does not think he can take another
emotional blow.

His dark heart longs for justice while repenting inside.
It is her evil ways inside her that still reside.

His sad look of destiny walks in the distance of fornication.
Yet, it was her fornication that spoke with eloquent desperation.

One soul that is dark in which it was left to ponder his realm.
Another soul torn in which it was left to wonder why she felt overwhelmed.

She denies her faults that reside from within.
He denies the emotional state that they both shared with bitter sin.

Her true soul she denies from being who she is meant to be.
His dark soul who tried to show her a better way, failed within his broken plea.

Emotional Demons

Running from these demons called emotions.
They leave me in emotional pain with dark notions.

They come for me with a killer's smile.
They look innocent but their intentions are hostile.

They would like me to hurt myself in the sense of no return.
It is these emotions that leave me eternally burned.

They have no self-implications of a haunting cry.
They wreck havoc on my soul that longs to die.

I am a soul that is intertwined with an emotional scorn.
I am a spirit that has been broken who whispers to mourn.

I try to do the right thing over and over again.
Yet I fail in my convictions as it has become my depressing friend.

I want to be left alone to die in my emotional cold world of doom.
I want to join my friends on the other side of death's tomb.

These Eyes

Through these eyes I have seen people around me bleed.
They create their own hell and prison unto which they plead.

Through these eyes I have seen people I care for drown in misery.
I can only watch helplessly as they turn blue in a black scenery.

I know they can live a better life in the life they live.
I know they can overcome and look at themselves and forgive.

For some reason through these eyes they'd rather live a life of pain.
A life that yearns for death and points towards others for their blame.

They poison their bodies so they can forget to remember.
They want to lose their pain that comes with the rain in each November.

I would rather them die on their feet with proud premonitions of a valiant defeat.
But they crawl on their knees for this life they long to forget for this life they will have
to repeat.

Me

I am alive but I am alone.
I can see yet I am blind to the fact.
I can rationalize yet I am misunderstood.
I can yell my plea, yet no one can hear my sanity.
My screams are not heard in a world that is morbid.
My wings have been clipped to keep me from flight.
My life is slipping away in the dead of night.

Author's Comments:

"May you find yourself again CalfCruncher"

Hollowed

I am hollow again.
A mere empty shell of myself that is my bitter friend.

I have been killed before yet I endured.
Yet this time around I do not think I can be cured.

By no means was I ever an angel in a black world.
My heart has stopped and it is my soul that is being hurled.

I can definitely take the physical pain.
Yet it is the emotional pain that sometimes drives me to insane.

My heart bares the scars of being crucified over and over again.
The only word I have left to say when I find someone is "When"?

When will I be killed again?
When will I be an empty shell that has become my close friend?

I'm Tired

Foraging through a rumble of misery.
It is the innocence that has forsaken me.

I am brandished a fool for all to see.
The rainmaker of sincerity has forgotten me.

My pain is immortal with premonitions of death.
It is the same lines I speak that are spoken under my breath.

I pray everyday that death rescues me from this lasting life.
Yet I am still here wishing I was in the afterlife.

My shell remains as my spirit is already gone.
My soul wants to leave as my demeanor has become withdrawn.

I am waiting to embrace the end of my demise.
My cries go unheard for my longing to die with the pain burning inside my eyes.

Cancer

In the eyes of the Jackal she bore the defiance of a Lion.
She roared with ferocity in her intent to become a daughter of Zion.

She felt the pain of the sickness that overwhelmed her over time.
Her battle was long lasted and it was her will that wanted to shine.

Her eyes gave the impression of a winner while submitting to defeat.
For her to have lasted as long as she did, she was noble in her feat.

She faced insurmountable odds.
I told her to rest and go with God.

I remember her last dy-ing breath.
The look she gave me as she submitted herself to death.

Tears rolled down my cheeks as I cried.
She closed her eyes as she transitioned to the other side.

Disdainful

She was an angel with a face of a demon.
Her wicked ways resembled the work of an evil mind.
She fabricated the truth of wisdom, which seeped from her fingertips.
Her smile was warm with deceit that hid beneath it.
She was a wild flower that had no consistency.
Her eyes were a reflection of desperation that yearned to be wanted.
She always used self-sabotage because she felt she didn't deserve to be happy.
Now her bitter end is heartbreak of misery being released.
Maybe she will embrace happiness on the other side.

Beautiful Disaster

The fire fills the sky with a red orange outline.
The beauty it brings is the false image of beautiful wings.
It rinses through our hope and extinguishes our dreams.
It fills us with joy while ensuing to destroy.
My eyes water with excitement of visions of burning skies.
My body burns to ash as this world turns into a splintering flash.

Dy~ing

I look beneath the depths of my soul.
A greater token for that lost emotional hole.

I am wisdom of eternity that seeps through.
An image of mortality that brandishes the fool.

A foul smell of hate that rises with the beast.
It is the sins of the sinner that has him caged awaiting the feast.

Anger floats in the air filling the void.
It is the pain that arrives that becomes destroyed.

Death is waiting as I dance under the moon.
I hear the hoofs of the four horsemen that are coming soon.

Fools

No repercussions for ignorant minds.
It is the fallacies they ignore and hide.

They assume we do not see them for what they are.
Amusing themselves with retributions from afar.

They seek attention at any cost.
Not knowing how well we know they are lost.

They speak with immoral demands.
Yet it is the actions taken that is soaked on their hands.

Floating through life thinking this will be the best it will ever get.
An empty cathedral celebrating a life of regret.

Agony

You're the one that can see the darkest side of me.
The infection that burns through your broken plea.

The envy that consumes you.
The rage that breaks in two.

Your demeanor is defined with an evil eye.
It is a heart that is felt that yearns to die.

My veins are ice cold with a butcher's smile.
It leaves me in solitude lurking with feelings of hostile.

You cannot break the ice with a pick that does not exist.
It is your irony of good that portrays its evil twist.

You are the dying maker of a good that went wrong.
Seeking my assistance in an effort to prolong.

Prolong the agony of going back to life.
This life to life less with a meaningful strife.

US

The white noise cuts my skin.
It tears it away with empathic sin.

I bleed the thorns of misery.
I ran into the mouth of sincerity.

I keep my mind open and pure,
to cleanse away the sickness for the cure.

My fingertips bring the chills that run down your spine.
Your image of me has become masterfully divine.

I am the soul that has been tarnished with black sin.
I am the strong spirit who brought you in with the push of the wind.

I tear away your emotions of sorrow.
You are me and I you with visions of a bloody tomorrow.

I seek the essence of the Covent of your soul.
I am the one you brought here to console.

Our tears of blood become one.
As a minister of faith we become undone.

Land of the Dead

They walk everyday in a land that does not see them.
They are alive yet they are dead to the world.
Their insignificance is unnoticed by society.
Every day it is the same routine.
Every day is their life for the rest of their life.
The dead alive with the living.
Trying to make their existence heard in the Land of the Dead.

Floating Through Life

Your lack of wisdom shows in your smile.
Your look is deceiving yet versatile.

I cannot fathom your life of pain.
Your masquerade you dance, to hide your gain.

Your human shell is a waste of life not giving it's full.
It is your mind that is deteriorating as you try to pull.

Pull insanity back from sane
as you try to act of the norm,
yet it will always remain in vain.

Filth Pig

Your face is filled with everlasting disgrace.
It is the sickness you embrace while losing the chase.

Your eyes bleed with deceit far off from the norm.
In comes the wicked winds as you welcome the storm.

The blackened sky speaks vile through your words.
They come running to you in masses and in herds.

At the wave of your evil hand, death begins.
The slaughter embellished displaying the pigs sins.

You exemplify a horrid picture of yourself of the graves you dig.
Yet what you see in the mirror is nothing more than a filth pig.

Mis~Guided

The blood red sky fills me by design.
It lacks me the desire to kill when needed to kill.
It drains me of who I am to be and what I am now.
My wings are clipped from immortal means.
This society wants me to bleed.
It is nothing more than a mal-nourished fool running through the streets.
I the prey in the realm of defeat.

Drowning Souls at the Edge of The World

Standing on the edge of the world.
It is the souls of sin that have been hurled.

The screams are heard through the realm of the dead.
Their life of sin left with words that are unsaid.

The foul smell of rotting corpses lay throughout the land.
It is their meaningless existence that was counted on their hand.

They speak no more of tainted sins.
It is them that have been forgotten in which their hell begins.

Their eyes reflect the pain they dwell in.
Their shame is their dignity in which they buy in.

They are forgotten souls that left with blistering remorse.
It was the meaning of their life that took its course.

Shadows Fall

Visions running through streams of sadness.
Embracing the emptiness with a stare of madness.

Your soft skin smooth as a tranquil lake.
It is this dark shadow that has re-emerged I cannot shake.

The pillager runs through with his murderous axe.
It seems as though I am on needles and they will not allow me to relax.

The face behind the dark shrouded hood is misunderstood.
I long from evil as I wish I could be graced with good.

The simple demands of life make it so complex.
It is the hard stipend of death that waits in mourning to snap my neck.

I succumb to the depths of the ocean floor.
Gasping for air as my lure is taken to adore.

Adore the whore of non-forgiving pain.
It is the masquerade drops that come from the black rain.

Sinking in despair with echoes of laughter in the distance.
It is the mirror of lies that threaten my very existence.

Empty Eyes

The glare of a cold stare brings the frigid ice.
It longs to burn with a menacing slice.

The only weapon you have is the look in your eyes.
Yet it only brings a cold feeling of a blackened despise.

No remorse for the whipping effect.
It is your soul that has been wrecked.

Your lips they speak of misery and lies.
It is your heart that has been broken with blood drip cries.

No more sulking for the breed of hate.
It is your cold stare that leaves you in a hypnotic state.

The only truth I use to know was the look in your eyes.
Now those eyes lie empty under a vast array of crimson skies.

Countless Act

Soaking in sorrow with a vengeful song.
It is the mortal sin that reminds me I have done wrong.

No more weeping to the endless sounds of compassion.
It is the mouthful of beatings that fill my ration.

One mistake and my life has been branded.
With a sea of fools I find myself stranded.

Running through mists of vain.
A seemingly endless journey of living with the emotional pain.

No matter how many countless good acts I have done,
I will be judged by the sins of one.

HaNgIng

I left my soul at the gallows pole.
It was my innocence they stole.

I wore my emotions on my sleeve.
My true intentions I conceive.

I run with the spirits that fly over the misty mountains.
They take me to the plentiful fountains.

My rage turns into pain.
My pain begins to drain.

My spirit runs free with the four winds inside me.
I give my lasting display of pleasure with my final plea.

Dark World

I keep banging my head against the window.
I keep trying to see the world outside.
No more broken glass I grasp in my hands.
The splinters are in too deep.
I cannot fathom this life.
It is this life that rewinds in my mind.
I am still trapped in the dark seeking the light.
I am tired of brick windows.

Nobody's Real

The perils of hell hound you in your sleep.
It's the demons footsteps you hear as they creep.

Your silence keeps your existence.
It is your cold stare that represents your resistance.

Your emotional torment is nothing more than your sanity.
It is thee acts of the butcher who represents the inhumanity.

Your fear is your oppressor of believing.
It is your dreams that mold the nightmares to their weaving.

Your life is nothing more than a pawn in a game with the dead.
Your life is pursued by the demons who will eventually take your head.

In the meantime you try to keep your soul by making no sound.
The life you live is taking its toll and it is the one that keeps you bound.

True Visions

These convictions are tearing me apart.
They are consuming me and ripping my black heart.

I can't see past the red sins that have been placed before me.
I can't run with shadows for fear of the blinding sea.

The thunder spreads across the gray outlined sky.
Its sound washing away the tears that defy.

Defy the master in his presence of frozen time.
A wicked blackness that accompanies the pain in his prime.

Watching for the killing fields as they burn.
Waiting and lurking until they yearn.

Yearn for the magic that exists in our minds.
Wanting the clear picture that holds and binds

Gone

I blow the red pedals as they fly away in the wind.
I know it is the front of deceit that she thought we sinned.

I reap the willows of death that rises above.
Another lapse of flight that was lost in a forbidden love.

The peaks have fallen from the earth.
The lasting time was well beyond my worth.

She has spoken her last words of two forgotten fates.
Her image fading slowly beyond the cemetery gates

Her love I have let go I do regret.
The love we engaged in I will never forget.

Torn

Love is suicide.
When it's gone, a piece of you has died.
It leaves your emotions being denied.
It leaves questions that your significant other keeps confined.

There is no truth in the game of love.
The one that was thought to have come from the heavens up above.
Is nothing more than a than cheap imitation of a white beautiful dove.
It is not them that has done you in, but the word called love.

It is a tempting fruit with juices that flow so sweet.
Yet it sours over time and some even turn into deceit.
In the beginning this word makes you feel complete.
Yet it leaves you empty with your head down in mortal defeat.

So I say to you all, love is suicide.
The mere speak if it is your finger on the trigger to which you reside.
Your heart has been pierced with a broken arrow unto which you have cried.
No need for violins in this demeaning saga, it is the word love that has lied.

IV. POEMS FROM THE DARK SIDE

These poems are very dark. They come from my vivid imagination and my creativity. These poems are sinister in nature and are to be taken for what they are and nothing more. Please read with caution.

Nightmares XI: Unsung

They have left me unsung.
I have been left to the gallows to be hung.
Bodies being broken on the rack.
Faces being stabbed in the back.
Blood dripping from their eyes.
The innocence is acknowledged and despised.
Their whips cut deep into my flesh.
My wounds seep through and the blood is fresh.
Limbs are being torn from their bodies.
I am screaming in terror as they forgot thee.
They resume the noose around my neck
and place me on the hangman's deck.
The sound of the lever is heard.
My legs dangle in the air as I am thinking my forgotten words.
My face is turning blue.
The rope around my neck sticking like glue.
My eyes open as I am gasping for air.
I am choking with a shocking stare.
The death of me was nothing more than a realistic nightmare.

Nightmares XII: The Suffering

The swift blow to my head
left me unconscious and close to dead.
I felt a tingle that ran down my spine.
It was their hunger that brought them to dine.
When I awoke my hands were bound.
They came to me as I dare not make a sound.
They grabbed me as I tried to resist.
It was useless as they marched me down the hallway by my wrists.
They gave me to a black hooded bastard.
He beat me badly as beatings became faster.
I saw him sharpening his white glistened blade.
I was beaten so badly my senses were beginning to fade.
He laid me down on a slab of wood, where my life took another course.
His blade came down with shining brutal force.
Off came my head.
Yet I was not yet dead.
I couldn't breathe as I looked at my body falling to the ground.
It was so quiet you couldn't hear a sound.
I awoke gasping for air.
Another realistic nightmare that left me with a bold bitter stare.

Nightmares XIII: The Reckoning

I have slashed my way through a crashing army.
The blood drips from my blade and the bloodstains adore me.
This brutal battle has gone on too long.
I have slit throats, cut off heads, limbs, and have committed an evil wrong.
I am cutting my way to their master so that this nightmare can end.
The screaming and yelling with clang of metal are dark sounds with a blend.
I have grown accustomed to the bloodshed.
It is their master I will leave with his head.
There is a dark evil in his eyes.
He will not go quietly for it is my blade that he defies.
His spear he runs through me.
I grab and pull my impaled self to set the combatants free.
Stains of blood are left behind me on his mighty spear.
The closer I get to him I can smell his fear.
I lift my blade up high as I am impaled with a painful sigh.
My blade came crashing through his chest as he died.
As I am dy-ing my army grabs the dead and burns them.
I am awakened with a pain in my sternum.
My eyes open to the bedroom wall.
It was a nightmare of a bloodshed battle and my demise as I hear my beckon call.

Nightmares XIV: The Demon Sent From the Devil

I could hear the tremble of his hoofs.
They came near with a surprising fear.
I could not articulate what it was as I tried to steer clear.
It sounded like a horse, but with only two legs.
It sounded like pounding with two pegs
as it came trotting through the night.
I became afraid as this was not a normal sight.
I could see the horns protruding from his forehead.
His teeth were sharpened and his yellow eyes looked dead.
He snarled with great passion as I ran.
The bottom of his torso was made of horse and the top was made of man.
I ran as my lungs began to burn.
He was right behind me with a solid pace that stood stern.
He threw me down to the ground with great force.
He told me that sin and I should get a divorce.
He said he had been watching me from afar.
His sinister hands picked me up as I was thrown next to a wooden bar.
He started laughing as he was gazing in my eyes.
His white shiny teeth were hypnotic as I felt mesmerized.
His gigantic hand reached through me to the other side.
He told me the other side was hell and that I should start to abide.
My eyes opened wide as my body was jerking.
It was another nightmare that left me scared and smirking.

Nightmares XV: The Slaughter House

There is an agonizing pain in my back.
As my eyes open I see I am hanging from a meat hook rack.

The pain is immense and I cannot scream for fear of them hearing me.
There is a steel beam that runs across the ceiling.
I pull myself up with both hands in desperation hoping they can't see me.

The hook slips out from my flesh as I let go and my body falls to the floor.
I look around and the bodies that lay on the ground must be here to store.

I crawl to the edge of the door and pull myself up.
The stink is unbearable and blood drips from a tin cup.

I easily turn the knob to open the door.
As it is opening there is creak and a man screaming and yelling for more.

Two men are systematically cutting another man apart.
He is screaming in pain telling them to stop as the other two are throwing pieces of
him in a meat cart.

I grab a meat hook that is hanging on the wall.
I swing at one and I connect with his head as pieces of him fly on the cutting room
stall.

I swing at the other and the hook runs through him.
Policemen burst through the door and shoot me with no conviction.

As I lay there gazing at the ceiling,
my throat is dry and my body has a cold feeling.

The sound I hear is the beat of my heart that is near.

My eyes open and I awaken to another nightmare that has spoken.

Laughing In The Mouth Of The Beast

Her fangs could be seen from the side angle of an adjoining room.
I knew I was in for a long night with a certain reek of doom.

Her wings began to emerge from her back.
They were twisting out of her shoulder blades
and I knew she was going to begin her attack.

Her benevolence was as pure as dark.
It was vile and it was the ignition of the spark.

Her eyes were blood red with a cold staring glare
She had no pupils and her sultry body was stripped bare.

Her claws grew out of her fingers.
The smell of her death started to linger.

Her bat like wings began to spread far and wide.
With a swipe of her claws she ripped my side.

My skin was dangling and the blood was dripping
as I dropped to my knees.
It was the blood from the floor she started sipping
with relative ease.

I knew now I was at my end.
I grabbed a paper weight from the top of the desk
and started to fend.

I bounced it off her head and it did nothing instead.
It made her angrier as I bled.

She twisted my neck breaking it cleanly.
She broke it carefully not killing me.

I was paralyzed from my neck down.
She started feeding from my legs that were lying on the ground.

I couldn't feel any pain, yet she was gorging herself with my body in a feeding frenzy
way.
When she got to my belly that's when my life began to drain
away.

I started to smile and laugh where I lay.

Tonight I Murder

Screams that howl with the wind.
It is the mocking night that is surrounded with black sin.

The warmth she poses keeps my insides fresh.
It is her divine notion that makes me wanting her flesh.

I keep close quarters and watch her from the shadows.
It is the midnight hour I hope to meet her in the wicked meadows.

I value her physical presence.
I thirst for the lust of her vicious essence.

Her aura is surrounded by darkness I know.
It is her sex I smell that I begin to show.

Her lips are that of a blood red sky—line.
It is my dark desire to entice her to be mine.

I promise she will be beautiful forever.
My grasp on her is like a prison lever.

At last she poses with her sensuous fire.
Mine forever, frozen in time with a killer's desire.

Wicked

My rule breaking soul is not yet out of control.
Dy-ing young today is far from fun.
I'd rather be bold and grow old.
The least resistance helps with my brutal assistance.
My predictions of life's endings are a demand on my dark convictions.
The light in the tunnel at the end is the darkness I embrace as a friend.
I consume the nature of distance between myself and the continual persistence.
The inevitable demise is the black source of surprise.
The sorrowful endings are here for the hopeful sending.
I am tired of slowing down and being thrown to the eternal ground.
I am the defiant one who reached his destination as an only son.

Angels & Demons Play

The smell of angels soothes my soul.
The bloodthirsty demons have dug their hole.

They agree on simple terms.
Both manage their eternal burns.

Their diversity is their vanity.
Their world is their insanity.

No sign of death in the lurking hours.
It is the demons that sit and cower,
for the smell of angels hold the power.

It is the sin they gorge.
It is the lonely road they forge.

It is the angels' dust that gives demons torment.
It is the good they flood that is dormant.

Their conflict resolved as friends.
This contradiction has come to a blinding end.

The Brotherhood

The Brotherhood of Chaos has laid their claim.
They are disposable soldiers in a disgraceful game.
Their discontent for the immoral has labeled them to blame.
Thee eclipse of their violence was followed by a circular black rain.
It was their misgivings that stole innocent lives just the same.
The fixation of bleeding hearts was never there to tame.
They were apprehensive of the evil notion to maim.
It was their evil will to drive the force into the pain.
The brotherhood was defaced and this disclosed their shame.
They vowed to one day bring back the pain
and any survivor they would drive insane.
The butcher's demeanor was their disposition of being vain.
The Brotherhood of Chaos skillfully playing their disgraceful game.

Kill Me

To Metellica's song "one"

I have awoken so it seems.
Yet I cannot see.
I cannot yell out to anyone to let them know my vision is impaired.
So it appears to me that I cannot speak?
Silence surrounds me, therefore I rationalize to myself I cannot hear.
My senses are gone except for touch.
I try to reach out with my hands to feel my way around.
Yet it is apparent to me that my arms are no longer with me.
I try to use my legs, yet there is nothing there.
I don't know if I am alive?
The last thing I remember I was in plane and I was shot down.
What is that!?
Someone is next to me?
They just touched me. I felt it. I am alive!
What has become of me?
There they are again. They touched my chest I felt it!
I am alive!
What is this prison that I have been confined to?
What is this hell that has branded me?
Wait! They are talking to me in code.
They are telling me that I was in a horrific plane crash.
I was found barely grasping to life.
They are telling this was 11 months ago.
What?!
I tap my head back to them and tell them thank you for keeping me alive.
Then I ask them with urgency, now can you kindly
kill me?
Please kill me!
Please kill me!
Please kill me!

I Just Died

I am walking in a world that does not give me recognition.
It is an assumption of misguided superstition.

Only a handful see me and give me a look.
I ponder and wonder what it is I took.

I feel like I have been banished from my own society.
It is the whispers I hear that bring the cry in me.

I am in a lonely scene.
It has been redefined and painted as a picture that is mean.

I feel like I am in a different world.
Trying to tell everyone I am here as I lay down in fetal curl.

Then it dawns on me and occurs to me in my head.
A soft whisper says, "You're already dead".

Mind Eraser

My fate is subject to falling.
I see a past life and in them I am crawling.

These visions in my mind are of black and white.
They are starting to overwhelm me as I try to fight.

It constantly occurs to me of who I am.
These scenes in my head make me believe I am another man.

This institution does not answer my questions.
They whisper in private as I tell them my confessions.

They have me strapped down constantly to a hospital bed.
I tell them what is going on as they tell me I am dead.

"This is not my life"! As I scream in pain.
I shout to them, "I am alive!", as I question myself if I am insane?

They just muster together again and whisper in vain.
A tear rolls down my cheek as I lay to them the blame.

I feel a shock from my head as I am starting to go under.
My memories are bleeding away as I ponder.

My fate is subject to falling
Repeat
Repeat

.

.

.

.

Selling Your Soul

Black demons crack through the earth.
It is your soul they look to take for their embellished worth.

They seek to justify their claims.
Your soul they rape with vengeance in their veins.

They corral your emotions for the taking.
And so goes your will for the breaking.

They break your eyes that are the windows to your soul.
In they march with madness of horror as they stole.

They break from your chest as hastily as they rest.
Your human shell depleted and dy-ing with the wickedness you invest.

They hover around so you can see yourself from the air.
With swift flight they swoop down to the crack in the earth without a care.

Your human shell is no more.
You have been taken by the demons to be their concubine whore.

Sinners III: Beautiful Sinners

The dead trees swing with death in their midst.
It is the ground that speaks with the undead below.
The wind screams with lost souls that went hollow.
It is the living dead in which the living that it follows.

The thirst of their blood cannot be quenched.
They rip the flesh from their skin.
They rip the skin from the bone in an act of sin.
It is their immoral acts they have been involved in.

They defy the Master in His very presence.
They mock Him with arrogance and vanity.
They taunt Him with swagger and insanity.
It is their ignorance that they cannot feed nor fore see.

They make beautiful blood red sin under a crimson sky.
They answer to know one nor do they run and hide.
Banished for eternal damnation for all to confide.
It is their mortal sins they embrace as God strikes them down as they die.

Sinners IV: Wicked Sinners

They walk with devious intentions of the cruel kind.
They whisper soft subtle expressions to embellish their mind.
They trap you with the sex they sell and the violence you find.
It is your emotions they play with, it is your emotions they grind.

They break you down until you're physically spent.
Their actions of evil leave you with an emotional dent.
They are not happy with your despair; instead your soul is their content.
It will be your self-disappointment that you will be left with to resent.

They spread their sin in a form of a virus from town to town.
They play with it, amuse themselves, and then spread it around.
They mock you, taunt you, and make you wear a sinful crown.
They push you in their sea of sin and then watch with a smile as you drown.

Beyond Brutal

Your ways are of the evil kind in which it has twisted your mind.
To the misery you are kind; it is the misery you find.

You like to play with it and spread it around.
With it you try to tear me down.

But you see I am not of the norm.
I am a soul that has already been deformed
and fore warned.

I deface your longing to spread your despair.
Your feeble attacks are provoked without meaningful care.

In the end I left you crawling on the floor.
You were begging and pleading to me, no more.

Yet it is too late.
Your soul I grasp with the embracement of your hate.

I like the fact that you have awakened your hate.
I smile with revelations that I have twisted your fate.

I gave you hope and then I took it away.
Now you are worse then when you met me
and you still want me to stay.

I laugh with devious intentions at my side.
You are another mind that I gained as it is the pain you now reside.

Your memory of me will never be faded
because I was the dark soul that left you scorned and jaded.

Pieces

Look into my mind.
Do you like what you find?
Pick up those pieces in my mind
before you run out of time.
Those pieces linger with each broken finger.
I am the infected cure and you
are the disease that is impure.
I am the touch that kissed you at birth
that gave your life meaning and worth.
You are a concubine of jaded emotion and decay.
You soak your feelings as a disguise to make your twisted play.
Did the pieces in my mind blow you away?
Did they send you to another world and keep your evil thoughts at bay?
Those pieces in my mind are another time that sent you into a devilish divine.

One Night of Darkness

Cowering in the shadows to be sent afar.
Running through the night by a guiding star.

Black as night with no moon in sight.
It is the witches and devils that bring on the fight.

The curse boils with the witch's brew sin.
The devil's hiss is heard with death's discipline.

They own the night of the eclipse.
It is their stranglehold on a one-night apocalypse.

The spirits are awakened from the undead.
It is the scriptures of their past they left instead.

The bodies are spoiling with decadence in a city of sin.
It is their forefathers rotting face they see by their next of kin.

The end of the night is shown.
They all crawl back to their evil black holes, which have been blown.

Their one night stand is over and their thirst for the living is quenched.
They stumble back into their death fold trench.

There's a Tree Growing There Now

A small man came to me with a butcher's smile.
His actions of slaughter were brought with great vile.

He laughed and snickered as he hacked away.
He left me with nothing as he hacked with a violent sway.

He told me to take the pieces and bury them in the dirt.
The body was grotesque and I felt an emotional hurt.

I was crying as I was to help cover up this small man's killing.
I was heaving as the smell was overwhelming and unfulfilling.

I threw pieces of the body in the trench below.
While the small man was down there,
I hit him over the head with a deafening blow.

I began to bury him and pieces of the body that lay in that hole.
One murdered for greed, the other out of anger,
only one was a forgotten soul.

Years have passed and there is a tree growing in that spot.
That one soul keeping it alive and the other I just forgot.

Black Fang

His eyes were glowing in the dark as I was looking south.
You could see the drool steaming and falling from his mouth.

He was growling viciously from an outlined crescent cave.
I took my position as I was here for a holy man to save.

He was stalking a holy man from afar.
He was using the sky to guide his direction from the North Star.

The priest heard the horrible howl in the black of night.
He was startled and began to run as his life was up for a fight.

The black fierce wolf began to stalk his prey.
The holy man began to pray for it was his only way.

He began to tire and he knew he was doomed.
So did the beast and he knew it was the holy man he would consume.

The priest sat by a tree and said out loud, "I know you're there so come out or let me
be".
The beast appeared in full sight and growled with hideous evil and it was too late for
the holy man to flee.

I ran as quickly as I could to try and save the priest.
The horrid sounds of flesh being pulled apart from the bone was an evil act of the
beast.

I could hear the holy man scream in horror and in everlasting pain.
The sounds would have driven any other man insane.

When I got to the scene the priest's throat was ripped from the seams.
The blood was stained across the countryside as it looked like a nightmare of dreams.

The body was still warm as steam came from the open wound in the priest's chest.
His heart was missing as the beast was gone covered in a bloody mess.

Diabolical Dragon

The black dragon snickered with a smile.
He looked at me and said, "Won't you sit and converse with me for awhile?"

I nodded my head and said, "Ok".
He started to tell me of this ancient land that was near a bay.

He spoke of the many fish he caught and ate.
He said it was man who startled the fish away and changed his fate.

He went on about his heart turning mean.
He elaborated and stated that he is no longer clean.

He said the new food for him was the villagers sacrifice.
He explained it was ok and that he never had to hunt again or use his claws to entice.

I was frozen with terror as this dragon stood big and tall.
His teeth were sharp and his claws were neither small.

He said do I mind while he dines.
I said no and he began to tear a man apart from the vines.

The man was yelling as he first picked his legs from his torso.
I could not understand him with the screaming and yelling that started to seem long ago.

He then began to dine on the torso with precision bites.
I had to turn my head as the blood became an unimaginable sight.

The dragon had pieces all over his mouth as his forked tongue began to lick it away.
He told me to forgive him for his brutal and vicious eating way.

He then laughed with a snarling smile.
He told me I could not leave as he would make this visit worth my while.

He told me to jump down into the prison cell.
I did and I found many men awaiting their term in hell.

I was another sacrifice from a village of the dammed,
as I heard the dragon's voice as the cell door slammed.

Murdered

Dizziness appears in my mind.
My senses are disrupted and my vision is not fine.

Pictures if my life flash before me.
A short existence in this world I foresee.

A transition of realms that bleed together.
Another life to live now and forever.

Eighteen visions of blood red
as I take two more bullets straight through my head.

Twisted Killers

Laughing as death is stalking me.
Yet on this day I will not die alone and let you be.

The blood is pouring from my mouth.
It is the internal bleeding that will soon take me south.

Your blade appears to have pierced my insides.
Yet, it is my will that will not yet let me die.

Your murderous ways are coming to an end.
I was your embellishment of a collaborating evil friend.

When I turned my back that's when you unleashed your
attack.
You had a knack for your devious ways, but it was your intelligence you
lack.

Your face is starting to turn white.
Now it is my dy-ing evil smile that comes to light.

You drop to your knees and you start begging please.
Yet the pain is unbearable and your life will soon cease.

Before you sliced me to ribbons,
the drink you drank was laced with poison in your
cup.
Your stomach cramps and your dizziness are the first effects that come
up.

Soon you will be paralyzed with no bodily control.
I am slipping away and so are you as we lose our souls.

I have the satisfaction that I murdered you first.
It is our roles of reversal that I reversed.

So in my solitude of waiting
death,
I laugh that we both murdered each other under my dy-ing
breath.

Killing Themselves

Half moons and deceit of lies that spawn butterfly cocoons.
Golden dunes of sand that reflect the time in my hand and the season of the
monsoons.

A pitch dark outline of a black cold sky.
Refusal of accepting the truth with a blood drip cry.

Reasons to assume a wicked existence.
The same reasons to make the distance.

Pushing away toxicity in the form of a confused and evil human being.
A demon spawned to cause imprisonment rather than freeing.

The evil that is spilled exists in our minds.
They exist in individuals who are truly blind.

The blind that feed themselves the poison so that they can slowly die.

Queen Of The Damned

I am on the side of the angels who thwart sin.
With a whisper you can make them sing from within.

Can you hear me walking over your soul?
Was it the pain and torment that took its toll?

You are the Queen of the wolves that dwell in pain.
You are in an emotional drought and it leaves you looking for insane.

No more tears for the brash woman who controlled her life.
The penalties are out and it is the cause of your strife.

I am here to take your crown and send you away.
Away you will go with the sinners in their prison that will cause your pack to go a stray.

Your life is slipping away into unconsciousness.
It is the light you leave and you fall into the darkness.

It was all because you wanted to forget to remember.
It was the horror you felt which came with each September.

Your dreams are your imprisonment trapped within reality now.
It is this hell you will remain while you take your final bow.

Killers

Stalking and lurking in the shadows before they unleash their attack.
They pull their blades from within and slice you in the back.

You will never see them coming in the night.
Before it is over they will be smiling with graces as you fight.

They love to give the pain when it is needed.
They will remove your heart, squeeze it, and bleed it.

These killers are of the suffering kind.
It is the torment they like to leave in your innocent mind.

The blood they grasp as it runs from their hands.
It is the blood they seek for actions of sick demands.

They are the cancer that eats us away.
It is their sick twisted game of murder they like to play.

Slipping into Darkness

To the other world

Surrender your soul to darkness.
Submit it to the lost abyss.

Find within yourself a bitter emptiness.
Try to harden your heart with a soft caress.

Move to the emotion in the gallows that reside.
Reside in a heartless fountain that is the black to which you confide.

Find the dark "You" that enters the world of illusion that masks reality.
Know the two faces that display the duality.

Another life that exists into the now.
A life that persists too allow itself to endow.

The ghosts that hide deep within.
The finishing touch of the skeletons that begin to dwell from within.

Running From Murder

I have been pierced with a knife.
I am running as fast as I can for fear of my life.

They are chasing me down to finish me off.
I manage to elude them for a while in a very small trough.

The blood from my wound has left a trail for my doom.
It is the blood that I lost that has left me to assume.

Assume my life will soon be gone for as much as I want to live.
These murderous bastards have left me with nothing more to give.

I am lying on my back looking up at five faces.
They are staring down at me with a look that disgraces.

Disgraces my dignity of helplessness.
They begin to stab me with a narrow-minded finesse.

My body being butchered for the taking.
Another victim being murdered for the breaking.

BlOod CuRsE

The thunder could be heard across the black sky.
The lightening lit it up with lost souls that make their haunting cries.

His eyes were of black outlined with white.
You could not see his true face, for if you did it would ignite.

Ignite the beast that was unleashed with horrid force.
He was a brutal killer for a feast that had no remorse.

He stalked his prey with quiet passion that got lost in the fray.
The hunger for the blood of man left his mind in dismay.

His fangs could be seen every time lightening lit the black sky.
His nails were long and sharp that over lapped his finger tips which he used to defy.

Defy God in his very presence with a vengeance with every kill.
He gorged himself with every body until he received his fill.

The lying corpses stood still in time.
The unspeakable acts went beyond the line.

He made sure they felt pain.
He made sure their souls were attached to his evil banished chain.

For his chain of souls was to lay blame for their demise in a world of evil sin.
He laughed every time he hurt God with a grimace under his skin.

Yet it was God that cursed him that made him what he is.
For this beast was his creation it was his.

Yet we see him every day.
He lives amongst us looking for his kill with no further delay.

Smiling While Being Feasted Upon

He was an ordinary man so I assumed.
But I watched him change as his human body was consumed.

His transformation did not seem real.
His claws started to pierce through his fingers as they were sharp as steel.

He started to scream in pain and told me to get away.
But I was frozen with curiosity and my mind longed for me to stay.

Horns began to protrude from his head.
His skin began to melt away and I knew I should have already fled.

Mammoth wings began to emerge from his shoulder blades.
His human form as I knew him began to fade.

His voice became a deep deafening sound.
His jaw grew disjointing as his old one fell to the ground.

His teeth became fangs as they overlapped his rough textured lips.
I knew now it was too late for me to come to grips.

I tried to run but this monster struck me down.
My back was torn clean as the pain drew me a painful frown.

I screamed out to say please no!
But it was use less as this relentless monster would not let me go.

He began to tear my flesh from my bone.
The pain was unbearable as I started to give an unforgiving moan.

He systemically began to pick me apart.
Gorging himself with pieces of me as he did it as a graceful art.

My life began to drain away and I became delusional with the more he ate.
I smiled to myself as I was his feast as it appeared to me my life be destined to this fate.

Them

Looking beyond the killing fields.
It is the sword that they wield.

They feel the anger that comes from within.
It is the spread of their hate that they are ready to begin.

They spread their virus throughout the land.
They spread it from just a shake of their hand.

The sickness destroys the young and kills old.
It is the murderous world that is filled from the cold.

They rule the world with a twisted mind.
It is the evil they brought to the grind.

Their souls can be found in the depths of hell.
It is their vile sound they make with a smile within their empty shell.

When Heaven Falls

I have waited patiently since the beginning of time.
I have lurked over your shoulder tempting you until your soul is mine.

My screaming whispers are heard during your desperate needs.
I laugh as you repulse the dirty deeds.

I smile to you as your soul ascends to heaven.
You think you're safe as you worshiped the number seven.

I still see you and your soul I yearn.
I will keep waiting until your soul I can burn.

Sooner or later all Empires fall.
That's when you will hear my beckon call.

For sooner or later I will be wearing the crown.
You will be worshipping me when Heaven comes down.

Author's Comments:

"As The Devil Ponders To Himself"

Voodoo

Whispers of conversations, yet there is no one here.
Your ears are deceiving you; so you say to yourself while tying to keep your mind clear.

A soft touch on your shoulder startles you.
Yet nothing is there and it is the questions you construe.

The whispers are back in forth in your head.
It is the spell of the vixen, which reveals the undead.

You can't tell real from illusion.
Your visions are of delirious delusion.

It is the spell you cannot break in an effort to partake.
Partake in a sick game of the supernatural you make.

The shadow that revealed his name with a soft whisper made you mad.
It was voodoo that touched you in an act of sin, which was left iron clad.

Avenging

The fragile passion that dripped from her sexuality lit the spark.
It was the spark in the dark that left a lasting mark.

Her grasp of her dark side motioned the graphic ungodly acts.
It was the pain and misery in her waning moments that presented the facts.

The unity was an unjust that left her blood filled with remorse.
It was a trail of brutality outlined with blood that took its course.

Her perpetual murderous ways seemed to never end.
Her pendulum of violence became her smiling friend.

She became a spectator to her own work.
The innocence ran dry as she began to lurk.

Lurking in the shadow of death while returning to life.
Her reticence was guarded with her sharpened steel braided knife.

Her subtle ways began to emerge within a vicious circle of pain.
Her self-restraint kept her mind pure as she portrayed insane.

She was quiet, yet make no mistake she was zealous and true to her ways.
She lost her way with retribution as it became the norm in her deadly gaze.

The Witch

Your lips they speak of death abound.
Yours eyes give a look of blackness with no sound.

Your long black hair is in the image of a witch.
Your baby blue eyes give off the look of a cold-hearted bitch.

I assume you are here to take me to the gallows pole.
For it is the gallows pole that you will attempt
to steal my soul.

My spoken breath to you is that I have no soul no more,
for I was a butcher of a long forgotten war.

You will see the pain and miles on my face.
My innocence is gone and I long for a better place.

Oh how I speak the truth to which you deny.
It is the puzzled look I can see in your eye.

Your beautiful red luscious lips I hope to touch with mine.
It is your beauty that I succumb to within that makes me walk the thin line.

So I say to you good luck for the taking.
My soul no more for a Witch who thrives on spirits for the taking.

The Traveler

Her teeth were white as snow
outlined with a blood drip glow.

She was a beast that was released from within.
Within her dark heart that reflected her mortal sin.

It was the human flesh she craved for in a most irritating way.
It was the bones she grinded with which she liked to play.

She was a creature created from the sin of man.
She has roamed this land since time began.

Her prey is the weak that falls behind.
She stalks them until they become intertwined.

Intertwined with the evils of this world.
She is the traveler portraying an innocent little girl.

Then her savagery is released and their vile
is consumed by the beast
from God's reluctant smile.

Betrayed

Mixed emotions in a devotion of truth.
It is the sins of destiny that reveals the proof.

Mystic Showers of pain rain with furious force.
It spreads throughout the realm taking its course.

A betrayal of hurt that was consumed by hate.
No more loyalty exists in the heart of lost fate.

A sharp pain that ignites the fire from within.
Actions that precede the consequences in an act of sin.

No remorse. No regret.
No division of suicide that poses a threat.

Treason poised with composure in absolution.
Elimination of the hurt is the murderous solution.

No Conscious

Your remorse is no more than regret.
It is your lack of guilt that has made you forget.

You are a daisy for the taking.
You are in emotional turmoil for the breaking.

You seek assistance for your efforts of dyer need.
You find nothing more than emptiness that you bleed.

You are a victim of a trueness of one's heart.
Your life you fear which you do not dare to part.

A seemingly endless journey of retribution with a killer's smile.
A path of destruction that whimpers malice that is vile.

Obsession

I smell your essence.
I seek your actions of dire consequence.

Where ever you go I will find you.
The black rose represents the death I construe.

Images of you are in my head.
They represent the actions I shred.

I will take you to another place,
one that represents a demons face.

You will fall victim to your convictions.
It is the manifestation of your morals that keep your restrictions.

You bow your head as if you already knew,
that the wings of vengeance were coming for you.

Life of Sin

May the devil find those who have sinned.
May he forever burn their souls and toss them to the wind.

May he take the arrogance they bleed and turn into pain.
May he bring them the abomination of a sinful stain.

May he banish them to eternal damnation.
May they bleed the sins of life in condemnation.

May their eyes melt with the burning of their souls.
May their life of sin break them and take its toll.

Let their life of sin clip their wings from destiny.
Let them see the true definition of a twist of irony.

Sin

Your future is my present.
Your present my past.
No more wallowing in the undertow.
From the tongue come words of living in oblivion.
A ragged drift of air burns inside my lungs.
It reeks the wicked that yearns to be undone.
It follows the heart to the city of sin.
It bathes while succumbing from within.
It knows no boundaries of action or faith.
It lacks the integrity of character and swims in shallow virtue.
It brings with it the suffering of wisdom.
It is here where it receives its birth.

You Can't Find Me

I hide among the crowd of illusion.
I dance with a smile while leaving confusion.

I leave a trail of littered bodies behind me.
They are butchered sadistically, systemically, with great envy.

I pick my next victim from town to town.
I make them tremble with my evil frown.

I am the affliction that came like a swarm.
I leave in the dead of the night leaving the dead in the storm.

I laugh with a crackle as the authorities can't find me.
I smile as I leave more bodies on my psychotic killing spree.

Falling

Uncontrollable urge of choice is taking its toll.
I am looking for the utmost satisfaction in making me whole.

Yet the necessary being will not let me have what I desire.
The revolution will begin for absolution of a maddening fire.

Yet the one who gave me choice has brought this upon me.
The choice for wanting more, this necessary being does not agree.

I have been banished, ostracized never to return.
I have been cast down and my beautiful white wings will now surely burn.

I have fallen, but not succumb to death.
It is the souls of the human kind I yearn under my breath.

Author's Comments:

"As the devil reminisces to himself"

Killer, With a Smile :)

He comes with a smile.
Hiding his intentions of vile.

You welcome his innocent demeanor
It is your life he looks to wipe cleaner.

The dagger he has hidden behind his back.
When you turn that is when he unleashes his attack.

You're being slashed to no end
from the killer with a smile who you thought was a friend

Consequence

This will be the last time I sip from your poisonous lips.
It is the taste I reminisce with the closing of the dark eclipse.

Your smell lingers in the air with the turning of the black sky.
Your eyes they bleed with every tear drop cry.

I notice the fear in your priceless face.
It is the embarking presence of a black embrace.

You fall beneath my feet and beg for your life.
A life without consequence is a life that bears a sharpened knife.

Your essence is of no more.
Your heartbeat dribbles away lying on the executioner's floor.

Forever Dark

The sun shines bright on this day.
The warmth is felt as I have forgotten my way.

Today I can see clearly beyond the self-inflictions.
I can move without daunting contradictions.

I feel so alive and pure.
I am accepting of this gift and this cure.

It has been granted to me on the verge of nightfall.
The gods of pleasure have answered my broken call.

When the darkness arrives we shall unite to transgress.
This will be a night of tonight-less.

How The Demons Died

The Lions roared with defiance in their growl.
It was the demons luck that ran a foul.

They smirked with arrogance under their breath.
It was the Lions jaws that proved to be their death.

Their wings could not save them on this day.
It was the light that burned bright as their faces were burnt away.

Their cries are heard today through the hyenas laugh.
Their transformation cut their black souls in half.

Her Dark Side

Boasting and walking as vanity is displayed in your dreams.
It is the repulsive scene that cuts the seams.

Your impurities have come to crow.
It is the seed you harbor, it is the seed you sow.

Your long hair touches the serpentine floor.
Your beauty memorizes as you play the flamboyant whore.

Your pride is the price you pay with your hidden smile.
It is the intentions of your emotions you place on trial.

Your hurt is never seen with physical eyes.
Only the eyes of the wicked like you can see with haunting cries.

13

Broken dreams of damaged tragedies.
Hidden agenda's and false fabricated scenes.
A mission of the holy to mend its ugly hate machine.
The evil comes as an angel with the halo that remains keen.
A false front that signifies its direction with the number 13.

A true heart can see through the darkness.
Yet that true heart is jaded by the black caress.
It is the vision of the other world that heart's witness is to confess.
This dastardly vision is aimed with protest.
It is the darkness this true heart tries to suppress.

Once innocent with the look of God from afar
Now tainted with evil in the distance displaying the fading scar.
The true heart wanders in and out of worlds that display its ruling czar.
A finder of faith that proudly displays its mar.
The number 13 that branded him to see the visions of the bizarre.

See Through You

I want to steal your salvation.
Walk away with your liberation.

Conquer your contradictions
and poison your soul with tainted convictions.

I want you to see the real me.
The butcher behind the smile of self-righteous integrity.

The one who brings your pain to the fore-front.
The one who longs to smell you for the prized hunt.

Your eyes are glazed with impurities that only I can see.
So that is why I am here to answer your unspoken plea.

Seeing the Other Side

Living in black rain that runs the insane.
It flounders in the light and flourishes with the pain.

The punishing beatings that are left are found in the soul.
It is death that brings the fear of spiraling out of control.

No love loss for the wicked sins.
No hate for the wicked to which it begins.

The black peril of the other side is a daunting vision.
Yet it is burned in my mind forever like a lasting collision.

Blinded

I need to run with dancing willows who are lost in sin.
Laugh with the jackals as they try to lure me in.

Their hunger is torn with madness that blinds them.
It is their thirst for my flesh that binds them.

One swift blow I control their fate.
I use their hunger to blind their hate.

I run with the dancing willows and leave the jackals behind.
Only to leave one while the more I find.

The Sorrowful Beast

The diabolical beast waits in his lair for his coming feast.
It is his season of the kill for he longs to cease.

His broken retribution of mutilation is the curse he must abide.
For it is his dark heart that lives and his pure soul that has died.

His sorrow for his horrid acts is his pain he delivers to himself with vengeful rain.
His tears of misery roll down his cheeks with the innocence he drove to insane.

This is his hell he must live for eternity with no shame.
Waiting to be released by the one who can reveal his true name.

What Was Once Mine

I asked for evil and she walked through the door.
It was her mystic eyes that left my conscious lying on the floor.

She told me she loved me liked she loved the dead.
Unfulfilling promises were left with me while I was left to ponder in my head.

Her smooth finger tips flowed over my body with an ease of pain.
She smiled with malice as she knew it was my soul she wanted to attain.

She was of pure evil with an angel's smile.
Yet I felt her bad intentions as they overwhelmed me with vile.

Her lips were luscious in the least.
It was the inner her that unleashed the beast.

Her intentions were revealed with a stab in the back.
It was her that left my soul feeling black.

She reached inside my chest and grabbed what was once mine.
An innocent soul that was to be sacrificed by evil's design.

6

The number 6 should not be mistaken.
Once it is recognized it is the beast that has awaken.

It yearns for your soul for the taking.
For it is the beast that comes for the breaking.

Its' glaring eyes reaps the wisdom to hypnotize.
It makes the soul full of lies and leaves it paralyzed.

It welcomes pain with loving care.
It hates with most precious despair.

It leaves a lasting impression imprinted in your mind.
It disdains your claims that stains the sins he will find.

The Devil Cried

He dropped to his knees.
He pleaded with ease.
His souls were of no more.

His heart began to freeze.
His dark kingdom held no more appease.
His soul shivered with the cold breeze as
the souls were freed from their beckoning pleas.

A whispering cry went fourth in the wind.
A blistering scream was heard with a grin.
A hell no more that stood alone with a lasting grim.
Once again he was shamed with a glimpse from within.

The Shunned

Falling into the heart of darkness.
It is a portion of evil in a hateful abyss.

Running through winds of black vile.
A spiteful imitation of a horrid witch's smile.

They bleed with an impurity that runs through their veins.
They squeeze the immoral and bound them with the demons chains.

They speak of an atrocity that comes fourth through their words.
They slaughter them in masses and in herds.

Their blade speaks with a swift blow.
Their actions are all that they know.

The blood drips from the mouth of the dead.
The seed that was sewn is from the disease that they spread.

Masquerade

She kisses a black rose as she dines on misery.
The expression is full with a touch of innocence.
Her stem runs deep in the mouth of madness.
She stands before me a wicked representation of black sin.
The petals curl up in a fetal position.
They embark on a journey of the dead.
The slit is made with a replica of death.
Walking into the shadows she becomes no more.
She is swallowed whole into oblivion.

Black Sin

The darkness comes forward to stake its claim.
It is reborn with ashes of the insane.
The sickness runs wild in the streets of pain.
The scorching laugh bursts the vein.

It's snowing in a time of righteous play.
The reactions of right wanting to stray.
They embark on a path of running away.
The scene is mean while waning in dismay.

Leaving a trail of white tracks in the snow.
It is the impurity that longs to show.
No one can see the realty of a stature that does not want to grow.
Disturbing behavior in the mist hangs below.

Wanting to get away from the forbidden fruit that tortures the soul.
A piece of the hate resides out of control.
Another beating at the hands of ones self who steals the show.
No more blood for the wicked, only a method to console.

Dream Evil

They hunger for their lapse of flight.
They imagine a fool that distinguishes their insight.

They fall to the Ravens who sing.
They speak of the time that was bore underneath the Raven's wing.

The eye of the beholder smirks with his vile smile.
He lurks with madness in the event of a lasting guile.

A black angel who spreads his wings far and wide.
In consumption of death is where he likes to reside.

A transition from good to evil over time.
This evil is withstood allowing him to embark in his prime.

A keeper who whisks away the immortal key to immortality.
A finder who ignores the scene of a dastardly reality.

V. POLITICAL POEMS

These poems are about issues that plague our society today. I do not take a stand but rather call it like it is and expand.

Reflecting While In Solitude.

The birth of the animosities.
The spawning of the atrocities.

The middle eastern sands
have engulfed the violence in their land.

The evil acts of evil men are the devil's work disguised as men of faith with despair.
They use Gods name to brandish their slaughter claims with no care.

The Eagle has tried to bring peace with its valiant flock to administer to humanity.
But it needs to fly back home and leave the badlands alone as they represent
insanity.

As much as it is our good will to share;
the evil is overwhelming and is leaving nothing to spare.

Many Eagles have fallen for a valiant claim.
They have given their lives for the innocence that live in the land of the insane.

Dead Beat Dad

He was a brash young man with nothing to lose.
He used the girls, for they were there for him to amuse.

He left the first one before the baby was born.
She stood quiet as anyone could see that she was torn.

He moved on to the next one in his life.
They had a baby as he abandoned them and left them in strife.

He got back with the first one and promised her he would never leave.
But once again she got pregnant, he left her in disbelief.

He found a third and she fell in love with his
charm.
Little did she know her new born baby and her would be left without physical harm.

Three women with four kids between them from the same dead beat dad.
They are intertwined in a twisted cycle that turned their lives sad.

Each woman knew the other had a child from him.
But they still took a chance knowing life with him was dim.

He was made from the selfish kind.
Destroying lives and living life in a tight social service bind.

New Hell Unleashed

You have released the demons from their empty soul.
They are flying throughout the earth to wreck havoc and turn this land out of control.

The whispers are screams that turn you green.
They disperse their venom that transforms our image mean.

Their evil laughs are heard throughout the land.
When you hear them it is too late as you are turned to sand.

The grains of sands that you walk upon are the bodies that once were.
They convert the land from white to black as it occurred.

The blood red sky falls from the rains of the human blood.
It is the blood of the innocence that floods.

Floods the gates of the portal that releases your soul.
A new hell unleashed called earth taken by the demons toll.

Drug Lord

I seek solitude in the confinement of my mind.
I wreak havoc on the pushers that I find.

Another day, another life is taken in my realm.
Life is not precious, nor cared for, as I overwhelm.

Overwhelm the competition with violence that is impressionable.
Make them think twice about coming to my turf making it irreversible.

I poison and destroy lives without a care.
It is the money and the high that gave me my cold as ice stare.

I push the drug up their noses or in their vein.
If they rip me off, I leave a nice hole in their head accompanied by a bloodstain.

I am the evil you see in society today.
I am the poison that butchers your family from day to day.

One day I will be dead, but rest assure there will be another to replace me just the same.
They will play the same game, yet it is only a different face and different name.

Tour of Duty

to my Father and my Step-Father and any other Vietnam Veterans

I have been placed in a foreign land.
The government sent me here as a simple man.

I have seen lives taken in front of my eyes.
It is this evil jungle that I have grown to despise.

I have become a proficient killer by my enemies' standards.
Yet they have also taken my comrades, making them cold-hearted bastards.

I kill so that I am not killed.
I was drafted and brought here passed through a congressmen's bill.

My life was a toy at the mercy of leaders' decisions.
Ideologies got in the way of human life and the governments admissions.

When I came home it was not a home.
I felt I was living life on a high interest loan.

They called me a sinner
and
an evil no good for nothing baby killer.

They spit on me in my homeland.
I was disgraced for being an honorable man.

The government sent me over there as a simple man.
Now I am complex with horrid visions from a foreign land.

Their meaningless ideology took my innocence away
and left the bloodshed on my hands without showing me a different way.

Opposing Hierarchy

To all the rebels in this world

Your hunger to feed your status has labeled you a loner.
You want to go where legends die and so you condone her.

She has left you and now your path is a lonely one.
Without her we won't save you and it appears you are done.

Your egocentric demeanor has capsized you.
Your self-centered ways have turned you blue.

Your savagery and pillaging are vile in our eyes.
It is the authority you ignore; it is the hierarchy you despise.

Your reckoning you thought would bring you new—found fame and glory.
Yet it has only foretold the downfall of your pathetic story.

You can run for the rest of your life, but it is your misery that you pave.
In the mean time I will the lay the flowers on your grave.

Apocalypse

To the world

Running with the Beast across the white clouds.
He is reading and screaming to me aloud.
The sky is burning with bright orange flames.
The fire falls down on the earth with fiery rain.

The mountains have been crumbled down.
The oceans boiled with evil abound.
The Beast has amassed his army of darkness to destroy.
To kill this planet of humanity and let it employ.

Employ itself with its guilt and hatred.
The Beast is smiling at the apocalypse that has been in-breed.
The killing fields are in full force with dire straits.
It is the beast's mandate of humanity's unforgiving hate.

Stained

The evil that men do is left unsaid.
In the graveyards the words are spoken from the dead.

They heed the seed of violence with repercussion.
They consume the madness of mortal disruption.

The ministry of pain has left its mark with extreme malice.
They have left it beneath the corridors of the dark palace.

Their suspicion is under a watchful eye.
It is their righteousness of life they deny.

They restrain from horrid pain stacking gains.
It is their ego that was lost; it is their ego that was maimed.

Their guard is down as they rip the nucleus of their soul from the human shell.
Forever they remain in tormented pain while being consumed by hell.

Vendetta

I am on a quest to achieve my vendetta.
They don't remember me, but they will remember my 25 berretta.

They won't know when its' their time to go.
I study their every routine until its time to unleash their death that will flow.

Long ago they thought they eliminated me.
Yet I survived.
They deprived me, humiliated me, and thought they killed me.

Now my thirst for their demise was liberated.
One by one I cut them down and through the streets it was circulated.

I was the ghost that came back to haunt them.
I even killed their families and their next of kin.

I wiped their seed from the face of this earth.
As my deed is done so goes my life's worth

I am the living genocide that survived a brutal attempt at homicide.
I am the soul that fulfilled another day, another vendetta in the life I confide.

Vigilante

I am alone in my quest.
I murder for freedom as the good I aim to invest.

I make your drug pushers, your pimps, and underworld bosses disappear.
I have implemented on the streets a new kind of fear.

Your murderers get murdered with no repercussion of consequence.
I give them pain and make them pray for death with chronological sequence.

I have no remorse for their decadence.
I have no regret for setting this precedence.

They reaped what they sewed.
Their destructive actions made them cold.

The ones who survive now live in fear.
It is my bold persona that will make them all disappear.

Iraq

Walking through a wasteland of pain and despair.
Mounting assumptions of repercussions and fear.

Visions of missing the total account that was lost.
It was the anger and misdeeds that were the cost.

A swarm of hatred that was bred in the tomb of the dead.
A picture of violence that fills the void in a donor's head.

The terms of peace are still left unsaid.
It is the politicians who watch as their people are being bled.

The sands of time are running through the hourglass.
The lives are pouring through into death in great mass.

Organized kaos rules the day in which it is to define.
Define the master's will to exploit and to defy.

Defy the scripture in which it is written for liberation.
Written in blood with an act of defiance with misgivings in desecration.

Insurgents

Blood stained streets with bodies that hang in defeat.
Mutilation is the norm with black sins of deceit.

Kaos rules the black smoke filled skies.
It is the violence that runs wild in the coward's eyes.

The price of life is nothing more than their gain.
The Eagle is trying to help as they are living in black rain.

No honor or respect to the gift of life that hovers above.
They seek death in defiance of the ghost that represents the white dove.

Horrific violence is on their dirty hands of sin.
They use God as a false image to justify their black souls that hide from within.

The Eagle seeks humanity in the land of the lost.
Yet the evil ones make it a place of fear that is lost at any cost.

The Middle East

An endless decadence of violence takes it toll.
It is the wicked sins that spin out of control.
The butcher of man lay dormant trying to make himself whole.

The fire burns from within.
It is the world of doom that must begin.
It is a region of turmoil that tears away the flesh from the skin.

They control the world with a twist of fate.
They spread their disease with Islamic fundamentalist extremist hate.
Humanity is what they yearn to desecrate.

No freedom of mind.
No wisdom to reap or find.
A sadistic region that embellishes the blind.

Author's Comments

"Birth of Civilization, what has become of you?"

Homicide Bomber

Lurking in the shadows, for the light is no more.
A replenished state of mind welcomes the burning war.

It brings the pain with exquisite taste.
It longs for suffering in a manor of lives being laid to waste.

It runs with the serpent's eye at its heels.
The punishment rages within as it likes the way it feels.

A murderous rampage in the name of one.
A butcher to some, but a hero to none.

A flagrant act of the malicious kind.
When he gives his life it is only hell he will find.

Death Row

Suicidal lies and eyes that hypnotize with haunting cries.
An apprise of freedom that walks with surprise while it dies.
The pain that magnifies with despise as it meets its mortal demise.
We say our goodbyes and hold on to our disguise as we try to keep the prize.
We decriminalize in faith of living a new lie in this life as we once again try.
We chastise and then we give our advice only to succumb to a compromise.

It is the death we suppress as we look to address a partial regress.

Inquisition

A gliding image rolls across my face.
It is a reason of inquisition that has placed me in this place.

I ask for mercy to the courts to find me innocent.
It is the disagreement of a partial descent.

The inquisitor takes me to a room of horrors.
They take the blade and butcher my skin as he exclaims he is the restorer.

The restorer of faith as he pronounces to my screaming in pain.
The pain is immense as I become delusional and empathically insane.

My bloody body is a corpse of lost faith.
I lost my life in the 14th century called Catholic hate.

Author's Comments:

"To the freedom to practice all religions"

War

To all who were killed in action

Visions that display maturity in its depth.
It was left with the death that was kept.

It found its mourning in its solitude of hate.
It was tainted with blood in the black of fate.

The reflection of deceitful eyes were confined to despise.
It was fused together in an everlasting gaze of demise.

I wept with crying widows who yelled in defiance.
It was this unusual vision that left a menacing alliance.

Women wrapped in black clothing stood in silence.
They formed a shield behind me to protect me from the violence.

Their faces bore the sorrow of raindrops of pain.
They screamed from hollow ground from going insane.

My belief in the acts of sin was nothing more than 17 standing visions.
Yet it was real as the sun, the earth, and my rational decisions.

It came to me beyond the war ridden ground.
It left me with a cold bitter feeling without making a sound.

Truth Through My Eyes

A fool's paradise appears before me.
A notion of beautiful essence I can see.

It is the mystic foresight that runs through the air.
It is the soothing sensation that I can't stand to bear.

Bring the pain, the unimaginable kind.
Let it rain with desecration so that it can coincide.

I have been branded a skeptical fool.
It is my heart that I let rule.

I see the false front that has been presented.
It is a thin line that has been prolonged to be banished and resented.

The people that stand before me cannot see.
They brand me, accuse me, and demand their fees.

Yet they are the ones who are bamboozled into this illusion.
I have been put away for speaking the rightful conclusion.

I sit and wait for them to murder the world.
A violence that is portrayed on the stage of a mural.

This prison is my freedom, which cannot be denied.
It is truth they deny and it is they that I defied.

Fuel

The hate brings the fire.
It unleashes a darkness that fills the skies with red.
The sun diminishes in its beauty with its orange flame.
The land resumes to black.
Faces resemble skeletons.
Bodies resemble bones.
Bones turn to ashes.
The world has been burned over.

Revolutionary

They have shackled me with hate.
It is their closed minded debate that will decide my fate.

My demise will be their relief.
I will fall victim to their hatful belief.

I have been outspoken and I have been broken.
It is these outcries that have left me here to soak in.

This reality is a premise for the longing of death.
It is these emotions I take in for my last breath.

A walk in the clouds of misery carries me to immortality.
Being crucified with no dignity for my teachings of morality.

Nihilism

An imperative world that screams irony.
A system that falsifies its existence.
An illusion of what is right.
Being blindfolded while relying on trust.
Accepting what is displayed in front of us.
Chastising the revolutionary who speaks the true word.
Nothing can be for real.

Execution

With a bullet in my back I tried to run.
Yet it was the ideology that made me the shunned son.

They pulled me back to the shooting post.
It was not something I fathomed, as I am not one to boast.

The firing squad began to load their weapons.
My heart began to beat rapidly as my truth was held as allegations.

My political expression has become nothing more than murder now.
As the soldiers pull the trigger my writings of freedom become my final bow.

Disposable Messiahs

The empty bodies felt like rain.
Fools run through a paradise of sin with no shame.

The soft whisper of truth that resides in the soul.
A beauty of disbelief that took its toll.

Life that is taken with the demands of a hidden entity.
A replacement of the word with the same old identity.

Don't let them reveal their name or you will burn.
Their twisted words they speak pressuring you to learn.

They reside in the shadows of sorrow.
Spreading their sickness until there is no tomorrow.

Empty words that pretend to heal the soul in desperate times.
One replacing the other as they speak their false lines.

Last Days

I say to you all, what has become of us?
From the moment of time we have long to lust.

Whether it is for power or for glory.
We believe in the power whores story.

Our world is crumbling right before our eyes.
Living out our last days, while living with despise.

No more caring in a world that has lost its soul.
This world has become a killing field and it has taken its toll.

We ride with vengeance in the wind.
The vengeance never stops as we have already sinned.

The world will end itself once again.
Yet we will not see it as our world will crumble with a fiery end.

Insanity Rules The Day

Death imposed upon the individuals that were left.
A presumption of an out cry of fallacy in its depth.

A far away wisdom reaps its gallows pole.
It is the sole individual's role that takes its toll on the human soul.

A wretched filth that covers the design of weeping widows.
A false front that displays the human eyes as the soul's windows.

Melted faces with flesh falling from their skin.
Their acts of violence are random and they don't know where to begin.

An unnoticed pain that inhibits sanctuary from the sane.
Acts of insanity that resembles horror's gain.

A corpse of rebels that run through the streets of sin.
They are screaming victory in the acts of their vicious win.

The lunatics are running the asylum they hound.
The sanitarium is inflicted with its own disease of insanity's sound.

When Peace Meets Violence

The knife pierced my side with vengeance in it's stroke.
It was the gurgle of the blood that started to make me choke.

I soon new this life would be fading away.
It was the peacemaker in me that got me killed today.

I didn't know it would end like this.
Laying here gazing at the sky in a bloody mess.

I try to stop a violent confrontation.
It was the swing of the blade that took my desperation.

The sky is turning black as I am lying on my back.
This life is now gone and forgotten from a brutal attack.

I had dreams of tomorrow still unfulfilled.
Now my dreams are of sorrow being slaughtered in the killing field.

BlOoDsTaJnEd TeArS

The glimpse of flight runs through the dark waters.
It is the siren sound that entices the dance from the devil's daughters.

The black visions of death that amount to resurrection in the flesh.
It is the soul that turns in the waiting moment to be once again fresh.

The sadness runs like a stream in an open field.
It yearns for the righteousness to be healed.

The madness fills the desires of wicked men.
It sets in and runs with conviction over and over again.

The tear that spills down my cheek;
leaves an oh so dark image that displays bleak.

The blood that spills is the blood that runs for cover.
A mortal sin of murdering the good brother.

Denial

Starting a submissive attack.
Running away until I can make my way back.

The mood that brings the pain
is the mood that welcomes the black rain.

Your smile is a fabrication of a false entity.
Your laughter is your delirious nature of losing your identity.

Your whispers are heard through a forest of sincerity.
It is your life that is slipping away with your clarity.

You find the desperation sealed with a lover's kiss
only to awaken to the serpent's hiss

The truth hides behind your fallacy.
It is the window that is broken in your false democracy.

Peace

Peace is a dirty word
It is nothing more than a mere word.
The definition no longer defines its' use.
The image has been faded and burned away.
It will never again return with a vengeance.
Peace has lost its' purity long ago.
War is the norm and peace is a dirty word.